Then the Angels Laughed:

A Landlocked Mermaid's Journey in Discovery and Healing

by

Heather Vaughn

Copyright ©2009 by Heather Vaughn

Editorial Supervision: Chris Lindstrom

Cover Design: Dave Clark

All rights reserved. No part of this book may be reproduced by any mechanical, photographic, or electronic process, or in the form of a phonographic recording, nor may it be stored in a retrieval system, transmitted, or otherwise be copied for public or private use - other than for "fair use" as brief quotations embodied in articles and reviews without prior written of the publisher.

The author of this book does not dispense medical advice or prescribe the use of any technique as a form of treatment for physical or medical problems without the advice of a physician, either directly or indirectly. The intent of the author is only to offer information of a general nature to help you in your quest for emotional and spiritual well-being.

ISBN

978-0-578-00986-5

Oceana Press

Dedications and Acknowledgments

I acknowledge all the angels and guides that have given the "push" and all people who have inspired and encouraged me to write this book and to never give up: Roe, Toni and Kayla Vaughn for being an amazing family; Aunt Barbara for being "Aunt B." and encouraging me to follow my dreams; Aunt Linda for always checking in on me; Nancy Clark for making me laugh and for always seeing the brighter side of life; Denise Dimatteo for always having me create something new; Chris Lindstrom for all the movies and good times and key editing points; Dave Clark for the amazing cover design; Tony Woodroffe for the commitment to healing with velocity; to the staff and program leaders of Landmark Education for their commitment to humanity; to my team of people- Kristi Sesso, Mary Icaza, Herma Schmitz, Margot Schoeps, Karen Teitlebaum, Glenn Cooper and Nancy Sloane for their ongoing support in having me be well; Angela Wurster for her amazing work and getting me in my appointments quickly; Joyce Pike and Paul Turro for having me be wise; Susan Marek for being such a good angel and putting up with my elemental side; Robin Reintz, Charmaine Blundell, Debbie Higgs, Kelly Sotomayor, Julianne Orren, Megan Harrison Edge, Denisha Dawson, and my many other angel and healer friends for the magic, healing and friendship; Mary and John Versosky for making Hawaii possible; Doreen Virtue, Angela Hartfield, and Betsy Brown for giving me the courage to spread my wings and fly; Cathy Simpson and Natalie Brundred for encouraging me to look deeper; Jan Matthews and my East West family for always seeing me as great; Diane Hasili for always believing in me; Dr. Anna Pavlik for believing in miracles; Ellen DeGeneres for coming into my living room every day and keeping me laughing during the week; and lastly, my mother and grandmother in the spirit world who are looking down on me with a smile

Foreword

This is my journey in knowing and discovering who I am as a healer, a teacher, and a human being. It is a journey in learning and working with the spirit world and allowing them to guide me. It is a journey in learning to accepting myself for who I am. It is a journey of surrender and allowing many people to contribute, to teach, to learn, and to love.

It has been a miraculous journey with an important lesson for all people, no matter what has happened in your life and no matter what beliefs you may have about the spirit world, healing, or life in general. It shows that you can overcome anything that life hands you. It also shows that you can be yourself and never have to pretend, hide, or adhere to someone else's standards or rules. Just be yourself! Follow your heart and follow your dreams.

This is my experience in my life dealing with the spirit world and trusting myself. This is my experience with trusting the world of the unknown and dealing with the circumstances life throws at you, the experience of growing and developing, learning to accept, and to be myself. I am an artist. I am a creative, spiritual person that denied that side for many years. I have learned to live life passionately and authentically.

There are many angels in my life, both in person and the ethereal realm that have helped me through this journey. I had to learn to trust and surrender to both.

While the information in this book is 100% true, I do not recommend using it to avoid medical care or as a substitution for dealing with important matters. While the angels will guide you and help you with anything, sometimes the advice of the medical world is key in your recovery. But most importantly, never give up!

I hope you enjoy reading it as much as I enjoyed writing it.

Chapter 1

I was about two years old the first time I saw an angel. It was one of the most profound and memorable moments in my life. I was living in Florida and attending a nursery school when I suddenly my temperature rose to 105* in a short period of time. I couldn't breathe. Light was swirling. Everything around me was getting dark and everyone and everything seemed so distant and far away. I was scared. What was happening to me? This didn't seem right. I remember being very confused. Apparently, I had a few convulsions and my father rode with me in the ambulance to the hospital. I remember the angels saying, it was not time yet, that I had work still to do on the planet. I didn't even know what that meant but I was comforted. A few moments later, my temperature was back to normal and everything seemed fine.

However, from then on the angels were always around me comforting me, teaching me and talking to me. I would ask them questions, play with them, create games and ideas with them and learn from them. It was like my own little world where I had the keys to the universe. I thought this was normal, that everyone could see the angels. If I could see them and hear them, then surely everyone else could. My mother simply thought I had an invisible friend. How cute I must have been with my big blonde curls and my big green eyes, with imaginary friends lined up like dolls on a shelf. Eventually, I stopped telling my parents, and anyone really, about my so called "imaginary friends" when it became very clear to me that they didn't think that what I was seeing was real.

I was always an extremely creative and highly imaginative child whose parents fortunately encouraged me to dwell in and explore my creativity. I learned to read books very young, at just three years of age; I learned to write my name in cursive before I was in school; and I could speak enough Spanish as a small child to carry on a conversation with an adult. This knowledge came from having a mother and grandmother who were both school teachers and a inquisitive mind that was eager to learn as much as it could. With a pad of paper and crayons I could, and often would, draw and color until the cows came home or until my parents told me to go to bed, whichever came first. I would sit and color for hours on end and be completely in my own little world. I would be totally absorbed in my drawings and not aware of the world going on around me. I would immerse myself in the drawings and loved to try to draw fairies that looked like the ones I played with in my front yard in Miami. Their fun and mischievous energy always kept me laughing and often found me creating mischief of my own. They were smaller, more playful and colorful than the angels that I talked to, but they were clear to me just the same. I could see them, and hear them like I could the angels, yet I could never quite capture their funky and extravagant beauty in my drawings. I was an only child at this time in my life, but I was never alone.

I have vivid memories of playing games equivalent to a child's game of "Ring Around The Rosie" in my front yard. I also would spend hours in the mango tree in my front yard talking with my "invisible friends" and learning from them what I could. I would create new ideas and listen to the stories that that would often send my young imagination into new worlds. Creativity always came very natural to me. Since I was an only child and had an imagination that was running full force, I often found new and ingenious was to entertain myself. I was perfectly content with my art supplies and was always interested in creating something spectacular. In the mind of a young and curious child, I was creating the universe.

I remember when I was about 4 years old our house in Miami was robbed. We came home and discovered it had been broken into. The house was in a shambles except for my room which was completely intact. I was scared. My safe haven wasn't safe. My parents were upset. The thieves had taken money, jewelry and my mother's cigarettes. I could not sleep. I remember Arch Angel Michael saying to me, "You are protected little one. Do not worry, we are guiding you." That was my first experience of Arch Angel Michael being by my side.

Chapter 2

When I was six, my parents separated. It was extremely traumatic for me. I wanted to live with both of my parents and didn't understand why I couldn't. I loved both of my parents very much and the thought of not being with both of them upset me a great deal. It wasn't until my mother and I moved from Miami to Memphis after their divorce that I began to get that maybe this being super-creative and seeing spirits wasn't a good thing. No one in Memphis seemed to see angels' no one else heard things, and no one else seemed to believe in fairies the way I did. I was in a new school, and I wanted so badly to fit in that I stopped talking about fairies and angels and the amazing world I had discovered. I kept this wonderful world to myself. This was the beginning of me keeping things to myself and not speaking.

My great-aunt Beverly had given me some Fluorite cubes that she had gotten from the mines of Kentucky. Fluorite is a stone that is used for healing and clearing energy, and I had jars and jars of beautiful green, blue, purple and clear fluorite cubes. I was enchanted by them. I loved them and was so drawn to them. These were my magic rocks. I filled the jars with water every night before I went to bed and would line them carefully along my dresser. Every morning my mother would dump the water out when she woke me up. I don't know why she did that, but it sure made me upset! She asked me why I kept putting water in the jars, and I remember saying that it was to heal and clean the stones. I think, instinctively, I knew to clean them, but to my 6-year-old eyes, I really just loved how they sparkled magically in the water. So, every night I put the water back in the jars and every morning my mother would dump the water out. Thus began my fascination with crystals and gems.

I really loved going to the Pink Palace Museum in Memphis Tennessee and looking at all the rocks and stones. My mother would take me often on the weekends. I loved putting my hand on the giant amethyst geodes and feeling the energy around them. It wasn't long before I could feel the different energies emanating from the different stones. This fascinated me. Sometimes I would touch a stone and I would get a short flash of where the stone had been. Sometime I felt actual physical vibrations as if I were holding a purring cat. Sometimes I felt a hot or cool temperature escaping from the rocks. Sometimes an intense feeling or energy would take over my body. Sometimes it would be hard to breathe. Sometimes I was compelled to place the stone on various parts of my body, often over the chakras. I felt that I had connected to a secret world that other people didn't see. I could engage myself with the stones for hours. I always loved experiencing the different energies that I felt when I was around them.

I fell in love with the stones so much that I wanted a clear crystal quartz of my own more than anything in the world. After begging repeatedly, my mother finally gave in and bought me a shiny, small, clear crystal quartz. I was the happiest little girl in the world!

I carried the crystal around in my pocket, in my backpack, in my lunch box; anywhere I could have it with me. It was my magic rock and to me, it held all the secrets of the universe. I would put it beside me when I read, I would instinctively put it in the bath with me at night and I would have it with me when I was worried or upset. I would play with it and include it with my Barbies, my collection of shaped erasers and my coloring books. It was always with me. Every night, I would put it next to my jars of Fluorite. At some point, my mother got rid of the Fluorite. I guess one morning she dumped out the water AND the stones. I never got them back and I was disappointed. I don't remember what happened and I never found out later from either parent what had happened. They are a distant memory in my childhood explorations.

Chapter 3

My mother was very shaken and upset by the divorce from my father. One of the main reasons that we moved to Memphis was so we could be around my mother's family. She wanted me to spend a lot of time with my grandparents and our other relatives in Memphis because she didn't want her upset to be the only world I saw around me.

I spent many weekends with my grandparents and often the afternoons after school. We made cookies and watched movies, and I loved going. It gave my mother much needed time to herself, and it gave me attention that I so desired.

My grandmother would have me go to church with her on Sunday's, and I always felt uncomfortable and totally out of place going. It never quite made sense to me. One Sunday, when I was about 7, I adamantly refused to go. I kicked and screamed and threw the biggest temper tantrum imaginable. I felt like the church did not speak the truth since they did not talk about the angels I had grown to know and love.

My grandmother was concerned that something had happened to me since I was so adamant about not going. When I told her about the angels, my grandmother, who was a fundamentalist in her beliefs, told me that good girls don't see spirits, and I would not go to heaven if I didn't stop believing in them. Well, that scared the living daylights out of me. I was shocked. I couldn't understand why something that felt so amazing and so right could be so bad. I was confused and didn't know what to believe. But, if my grandmother said it, I figured it must be true. So I tried to push that world away even though it felt weird to do so. When the spirits and angels showed up, I often hid under the covers and said "go away." The sense of peace and wonder I had gotten from them in the younger part of my life, was gone. Ultimately, I refused to attend church anymore. I could not take it. I may have been seven, but I was strong in my beliefs. Fortunately, my mother supported me in my decision. Although she encouraged my religious upbringing, she also wanted to give me the choice to follow my own beliefs.

While I was spending time with my grandparents, my mother immersed herself in many things and many new people to expand her horizons. Some of the activities were to keep her mind off the divorce and others were to connect with her own spiritual side. She took art classes, cooking classes, macramé, and Reiki.

Reiki is a Japanese form of energy healing that is also good for stress reduction. It consists of laying hands on or around the body to move and remove energy blocks. The premise is that "life force energy" flows through us and is what causes us to function. If our "life energy force" is low than we often feel stressed or get sick. If our "life energy force" is high, we feel alive and vibrant. She took courses to keep her life energy force balanced and not so much for the purpose of pursuing a career.

I remember her going to her Reiki class and coming home and practicing Reiki on me. I could see the energy coming from her hand, and I was fascinated by the color and the movement of the energy. I got excited when she went and was eager to see the energy when she got home. I began to mimic her movements and soon saw the energy coming from my own hands. My mother was concerned and told her teacher about my abilities to see the energy. She took me to one of her classes whereupon her teacher was stunned that someone so small could understand the world of energy. I was "attuned" to Reiki and I was only 7 years old.

Reiki attunements are what gives people access to receive the Reiki healing and give it away. I could put my hands on things: animals, plants, and people, and feel the heat and the energy radiating from them. This began my life as a healer. I secretly kept exploring this wonderful world of healing energy and by the age of 14, was declared and attuned a Reiki master by a Reiki master/teacher/mentor.

Because I was growing up in Memphis, Tennessee in the 1980's, this wasn't something to speak casually about. No one understood what Reiki is, and when I did mention it or the subject came up, people poked fun at it. Like so many other things, I soon learned to keep it to myself.

My teen years were just as turbulent as any normal teen's years are. I was a cheerleader, trying to fit in, boy crazy and hating the conventional education that was being offered. Even at that age, I loved to learn but thought the teaching methods were out-dated and boring. Our cheerleaders were always top in the nation and were even on the CBS news magazine 2020. We ruled the school. We also practiced harder than anything I have ever experienced since. I really liked the competitive side of it. I loved the thrill of the competition, the rush and the experience of victory as our names were called out as the champions. I loved that overwhelming sense of accomplishment and hated defeat. But as far as operating in the status-conscious world of cheerleaders and football players, I wasn't into it. I really liked being around lots of different kinds of people and had friends in many circles.

Pretty much that was my life at the time. Going to football and basketball games, cheering in competitions and dating, left me little time to experience and explore the world of spirituality. I knew I was a healer but couldn't talk about it. I could see angels but was afraid I would go to hell if I mentioned them. It left me very suppressed in the world where I so wanted to belong, and caused me to seek out other ways to appease my mind. When I was 16, Bradley, a boy that I had dated some, was killed in a car accident. This was very shocking and upsetting to me. The night he was killed, I was staying at a friend's house and I had a dream in which I saw a car hit a tree and he was in the car and was killed. I bolted awake early in the morning and saw a green flash of light go through the room. I found out later in the morning that the time I had awakened, was just about the time he was killed.

I was devastated as you could imagine. I loved him as much as a 16 year old could love someone. But what I was most devastated about was the fight we had had the day before he was killed. We had gotten into an argument and I had said some mean things which I really regretted. I had intended to apologize the next day but it was too late. I learned a powerful lesson: Say only what I really mean. None of us can be certain of what will happen in the future, and we may have no second chance to fix something that we might later regret.

Luckily for me, he came to me in a vision the night after his funeral. This was the first "visitation" I had had in years. In the dream, he was very peaceful. We went for a walk and sat on a park bench by my house. I was wearing my nightgown in my dream and he was dressed all in white. He wanted me to know it was not my fault and that he would always be with me. I could feel his energy. I could hear his voice, and I could feel his touch. It was as if he were sitting beside me in the physical world. He was well loved by many and missed by all. His death impacted a lot of people. I didn't know what I was more grateful for, the visitation or the relief that I was not to blame. It is the first time I remember speaking with someone who had passed. This was also the first of many visitations and premonitions I had regarding people passing.

Again, I kept his visitation to myself except for a few close friends and my mother. I didn't want people to think I was crazy. I didn't even write it in a journal, because I was afraid someone would find it. All I had was my memory of the visitation and how healing it was.

My mother was an amazing woman and she was gifted in many ways. She brought humor and laughter to many situations and was totally understanding in my loss of Bradley. I got many of my creative abilities from her. There was a lot in my secret world I could talk to her about such as Reiki, and a lot I couldn't talk to her about. I suspected that she had clairvoyant tendencies of her own but chose not to use them. She also told me stories of various relatives with psychic abilities. These abilities were never discussed in our family. I always wanted to know more, but everyone was totally evasive in regard to any of my questions.

It was really tough growing up in a world where I couldn't fully speak about my experiences. I adapted and became a "normal" teenager with a lot of friends and crazy moments. But for the most part, I never felt understood. I felt alone and never felt like I could just be me. Who was I anyway? I began to think I was some sort of freak. I felt like I was always pretending since I was intentionally hiding an entire part of me that no one ever knew.

Fortunately, I never turned to drugs or alcohol for relief. It just never appealed to me. Of course I had some drinks on the weekends as many teenagers do. I would go out and stay at friends and explore a life of partying. In college I tried smoking pot, drank a lot of alcohol and beer, partied like you would expect a college student away from home to party, but never got to a point where I was out of control. I didn't actually like the way pot or alcohol felt to me energetically, so I ultimately in my adult life, I stopped, except for an occasional glass of wine or so here and there.

As I grew older and became more independent, I started to reconnect to this past that continued to haunt me. I longed for this beautiful metaphysical world to be a part of my life again. Growing up in the south in the heart of the Bible Belt, with its super conservative relationship to religion and the spirit world, left me so unexpressed and angry. I unknowingly had let myself be suppressed for so many years. I knew it was time to leave.

Chapter 4

Another side of my younger years was spent being very involved in the performing arts. I started dance lessons before the age of 4, I took acting classes and voice lessons and performed in numerous plays, commercials and television spots and even did a musical tour. I, like many young girls, had visions of being a starlet in a movie.

When I was 19 I auditioned to be a performer at Disneyland in California. I got the job, and after my freshman year of school ended in May, I drove across the country to California with my father to begin a two-season stint with Disney. I was determined to be a performer and, being a huge Disney fan, I was excited and thrilled at the chance to work there. It was a dream come true for me. I had always been fascinated by the imagination of Walt Disney and was jumping for joy at the opportunity to experience it from the inside. It was my first time really experiencing my true independence and I took every opportunity I could to explore it fully. I partied often, went to Mexico on whims and played at Disneyland. I had many boyfriends at that time. It was a great time to explore who I was and to have fun. It was as if something inside of me was getting released. Although I went out there supposedly to focus on my performing career and expand my resume, I spent most of my time having fun, having wild and crazy adventures and enjoying my new friends. When I wasn't working or partying, I spent a lot of time at the beach. The ocean was always welcoming to me and had been a sacred place for me ever since I was a small child living in Miami. The days at the beach were my favorite, and I looked forward to walking in the sand with the water running over my feet. Some days I spent the entire day there and let the sun and the water sweep me into another world. I sat and daydreamed and at times could be a million miles away. I dreamed of a house overlooking the ocean, about my future as a movie star and what it would be like to have all that fame and glitter. I imagined worlds unknown and the vast mysteries of the sea and of the universe. Space intrigued me as well as the mystery of what lies at the bottom of the sea. Sometimes I read a book, sometimes listen to music, other times writing or drawing would provide a creative outlet. Sometimes a walk along the beach was the perfect thing to do and other times I would take a lazy nap in the soothing sun. It didn't matter to me. As long as I was near the water, all was well with the world. Often I might be out there from early in the morning until the sun set, its beautiful orange and red colors painting the horizon. The ocean felt like it was a part of me. When I was there, I had few concerns.

After my second season with Disney, I decided it was time to get "serious" and to focus on school to get my degree in theatre. In 1994 I graduated at the age of 24 from the University of Montevallo with a Bachelor of Fine Arts. I was a graduate, THANK GOD! It was a day that had been long in coming, and I felt an overwhelming gratitude that I was complete with it!

In pursuit of a performing career, I did a lot of summer stock theatre and regional theatre, and in the summer of 1994 I was chosen to work with a theatre in North Carolina. It was interesting times being around such artistic and creative people who were so self-expressed. These people were amazing and were hip and cool in so many ways that it was like a breath of fresh air. People wore crystals around their necks because it was trendy, and the thing to do. It gave me hope that soon people would see what I saw in crystals. By this point in my life, I had quite a few crystals that I adored, although they were mostly hidden and kept secret. I had decided that I would bring some of them out to "test" the waters. Since other people were doing it, I thought I would be able to do it too. I was relieved to find that no one questioned me about them and it began a whole new exploration of the crystals, their powers and how they could enhance my life. I was naturally starting to get back to the world of the mystical.

The summers that I spent performing with the North Carolina theatre were magical and not only because of what happened on stage. We were lodged on an old Indian burial ground on the bay in Manteo, North Carolina, so you can imagine the things a young open mind would see.

Manteo is also the home of an outdoor drama called "The Lost Colony." This area was one of the first places Europeans attempted to colonize America - 100 years before Jamestown. I remember walking among the ruins that were left by Native American Indian tribe, and I always had the experience that someone was watching me. Many times I found myself looking over my shoulder or feeling like I should hurry along. I got used to seeing spirits of deceased English and Native Americans and feeling their energies in the woods, down by the ocean and in my apartment. It was common to see odd things happen after a performance. Most of the time we attributed it to the large amount of alcoholic beverages that we were consuming. But then things began to happen even when there wasn't a trace of alcohol. After awhile these kinds of experiences became normal for me at this time in my life, even though I was still somewhat apprehensive about seeing these spirits. My grandmother's words continued to haunt me. "Good little girls do not see spirits." Nonetheless, I would wake up in the night and see spirits sitting on my bed, filling my room and moving things around the house. I would see an alarm clock's hands spinning and going crazy, TV remotes moving across the room, and the deep gaze of spirits of those long gone staring me in the eyes. I was terrified and curious at the same time. Even though I was afraid, I always called on the angels to help and protect me, and they always did.

Despite the many images and visions that would miraculously appear, the ability to see, hear and sense them was both confronting and confusing. I so wanted to be part of that spirit world and yet, I had my ego and reputation to protect. I didn't want my theatre friends thinking I was crazy. So I was comforted and intrigued by the discovery that they were seeing things too.

As in California, I also spent a lot of time at the ocean in North Carolina, drawing, writing and meditating. I wasn't meditating on anything in particular; I was just sitting and calming my mind. There was often a lot going on in my mind for me to calm. I couldn't explain it. There was something about the peacefulness of the ocean that just kept me going, even in the toughest times. It beckoned to me and always drew me in. I could go there and escape the stressful and often confusing life I was experiencing. As I said before, I have always been drawn to the ocean and have always been amazed at the vast mysteries that the ocean holds. I would tell the ocean my stories, my fears and my dreams. Every time the waves were swept back out to sea, so were my concerns. I could and often did spend every free moment there. Sometimes I would go by myself at night and stare longingly into the glistening moonlight and feel so safe, so protected, so understood and so at home.

The moon has also always been a part of my life. I would go out every night when I was little and look at the moon before going to bed. It was a ritual for me. There was always something about the pureness, the energy and the beauty of the moon and the stars.

I could gaze at them forever – the ocean, the moon, and the stars. There is so much being told by them and so much I continue to learn from them.

I have amazing memories of spending time with the ocean. I longed to just swim with the fishies and dolphins and immerse myself in the deep blue waters of the magical, mysteries of the ocean. I fantasized about being a mermaid and began having visions and, dare I say it, memories of days in past lives. I could disappear in that fantasy for a while only to be brought back to reality by distant screams of laughter from children.

The subject of Atlantis became a favorite of mine to research, study and learn. I often went to the local bookstore to find anything I could about Atlantis and Lemuria. It was a world that made sense that I longed to be a part of. This provoked some dreams that reminded me of visions that I had as a child, visions that I had forgotten and was slowly starting to remember. I dreamt of giant crystal spheres with blue and green and purple energy lines going back and forth. These lines formed a kind of grid or web over and around the crystal sphere. I dreamt of bright blue waters and the most beautiful and spectacular scenery filled with trees, flowers and animals. I dreamt of beautiful, loving and powerful people. I dreamt of dolphins speaking to me and swimming with me and teaching me many lessons. Those dreams became a huge release of energy and invigorated my mind. I longed for those dreams at night and would revisit the ocean during the day.

Little did I know how important the ocean would become as a healing ground and a sacred sanctuary for me later in life.

Chapter 5

Over the next several months, I did what I needed to do to further my career in showbiz. I was cast in shows, I toured, and prepared myself for the big leagues. I knew it was time to move to New York when I was on tour and this loud and profound voice said. "You should move to New York. You are ready". I had this thought and heard this voice over and over. I contemplated what to do. I asked the angels for a sign, and while I was enjoying a milkshake and cheeseburger, the powerful sound of Frank Sinatra singing New York, New York came through the speakers. I knew that the angels were guiding me once again into the next chapter of my life. So I took a deep breath, packed my bags and in the summer of 1995 when I was 25, moved to New York City. The Big Apple.

I moved there with the dream and ambition of pursuing a career in acting. As I said before, I had done some things in the past, commercials, musicals and such and had always wanted to be a villain in a daytime soap opera as well as tap my troubles away on the Broadway stage. While I did land some acting jobs, I never felt completely fulfilled by them. I was always trying to get somewhere, do something, and there were eight million other blonde-haired, green-eyed women who looked just liked me. Plus the idea of starving myself and eating very little to fit into the box called "uber-thin" really bored me. I love chocolate too much and wasn't quite ready to give it up! I knew there was much more to this but wasn't sure what. I had always loved performing and being the center of attention, from my young childhood days being an only child to the intense competitions of my cheerleading days. I loved (and still do love) being in the limelight. It gave me power. It gave me confidence and it gave me something to strive for.

When I wasn't auditioning, working as a waitress to avoid the starving artist syndrome, or reveling in the amazing sights and sounds of New York City, I spent my free time reading, researching, learning and understanding who I am and gathering as much knowledge as I could muster about the world that exists beyond the world we know. I became more and more fascinated by what I was reading and even totally excited by the fact that there were many people who thought like I did.

I began to expand my collection of crystals and stones, and I began to study, learn and use oracle decks as well as practice yoga. I befriended people who introduced me to Buddhism and the many deities of Hinduism. I learned more about energy healing. I learned about the chakra system and how to use it to create balance in my life. I learned about the principles of the Law of Attraction and how to manifest things rapidly. It was a very natural thing for me to immerse myself in this world, and all of it just made sense. I felt like there was a part reawakening that had been dormant for so long. I was drawn to study and learn more. I fell in love with the power of essential oils and the amazing relaxation and healing that comes with them. Candles were magical and healing. Life was good. I was happy.

My friend Cathy was a guiding light in my journey on my spiritual path. She was one of the first people that I felt I could trust with my experiences and with my fears. We were talking one day, and she looked at me and said, "Oh, my god! You are a channel. You channel angels." I didn't know whether to be relieved or terrified. Someone had come out and said something that I had been not only hiding but also resisting for a long time. I kind of sat there dumbfounded for a moment not sure what to say. So I said nothing.

I gradually began exploring my connection with the angels again and the power of crystal healing. I began to regain the confidence I had once had when I was a little girl before my grandmother's haunting words had created so much uncertainty and so much fear in my life. Nothing bad was happening in this world of the spirits and healing; instead good things started happening. I began to trust myself again. I began to speak more and more to the angels and ask them for help. I knew that even though I had tried to shut them out in the past, they had always been there and helped me when I needed them. I was grateful that they had not given up on me and had continued to bless me in the ways that they had. It was comforting to know that despite my "ignoring" them except for moments of fear, they were more than willing to pick up where we had left off. They were still willing to help me expand and reconnect with this new found knowledge.

Over a period of time, the "secret" world I had been hiding was out and what was so great was I had a friend who thought it was awesome. She really encouraged me to keep exploring and keep telling the truth about who I was. As I gained confidence around her, it became easier and easier to start speaking about my abilities to others. I began looking for light-minded and like-minded people.

Chapter 6

In my research and in my quest, I found out about people who were called lightworkers. I studied it, read about it and found ways to comprehend all this information I was being given. The internet was just becoming a phenomenon and I was putting it to the test. I stayed up late at night reading all I could about this lightworker person. I was intrigued by what I read and it resonated with me. It didn't take long before I realized that I was a lightworker who was in the process of waking up. A lightworker is someone who volunteers to come to earth to heal, teach and help the earth and its inhabitants. A lightworker could have many professions, such as teacher, healer or doctor. A lightworker is also someone who has had some sort of intuitive or psychic connection and perhaps someone who is here to awaken and empower the planet. This sounded like me. I wanted to learn as much as I could. I was excited about my new passion. The more I studied, the more I began to have dreams and visions of opening a healing and spiritual center to teach people about who they are.

I also discovered Indigo Children about the same time and, suddenly, my life made so much sense. It was like a giant magnifying glass was shining down on me. Indigo Children are people who are highly sensitive, highly creative and intuitive, and who are often misunderstood for various reasons. The more I read the more I wanted to read. All the conversations with angels, all the curiosity and being drawn to heal and to work with crystals, all the creativity, all the suppressed and often unexpressed anger FINALLY made sense.

Researchers have shown that, while there are some Indigo Children that were born before 1976, most Indigo Children were born between 1976-2006. I was born in 1970 so I looked for people my own age that had similar qualities. I looked for like-minded people that I could inquire with, learn from and share my experiences with. I discovered something called an Indigo Scout, a person my age or older who was sent here to pave the way. I met people who had similar experiences, who validated that, indeed, I was not crazy. My experiences and talents became something I could be proud of and not something I had to hide.

As I sought out other Indigo Adults, I also found many other lightworkers and other kinds of healers -- people who had similar interests as I did. It was great to know that I was not alone on this endeavor and that I could share my experiences without being judged. For the first time in my life, I felt understood and that what I wanted to do with my life made sense.

While I still was somewhat hesitant at this time to speak about things such as angels, crystals and healing, I did open up slowly to some people. My friend Cathy had created something when she said that I was a channel. Little by little, I began talking more; and little by little, I had several friends I could share with. My friends Natalie and Cathy knew the most about me. They encouraged me to keep exploring more deeply and to keep letting go of my fears. It was such a relief not to have to hold this in anymore. I had no idea how much I had kept silent and how much I had locked away.

It was also at this time in my life when I began a series of transformational programs. I was really out to discover who I was. I let go of a lot of anger and fear that had been building up in my life and began truing up to who I am.

Throughout this incredible process, I learned how to make extraordinary things happen in my life and in the lives of others. I began to understand the power of intention and how to create things around me. I began using my new knowledge with the things I had uncovered such as the Law of Attraction. I became clear that I wanted to make a difference at a global level and that I was a leader. I jumped in and absorbed as much of this as I could and ran with it. I had never considered myself a leader. To me, I was always the odd one out. But looking back, I seemed to always have plenty of people around me, following me and asking for guidance. Other people consistently saw me as a leader, and, I guess, it was time for me to get I was a leader.

Chapter 7

During this period of my expanded growth and transformation, my mother became very ill. She was having continual bouts with bronchitis and was coughing all the time. After several pleas to see a doctor, she was diagnosed with a tumor on her lung and surgery was needed to determine whether it was benign or malignant. During the surgery, it was determined that it was indeed lung cancer, and a large portion of her lung was removed. This happened a week after Thanksgiving when I was 27. I was very grateful for all the work I had been doing to let go of anger and fear. It gave me power in healing myself, forgiving myself and completing things with my parents.

My mother had been a smoker all my life despite my urgent pleas for her to stop. She was a teacher in Mississippi and during her illness we found out just how well-loved she was by her fellow teachers and students. They went out of their way to make sure she was comfortable and had all she needed, which was great since I lived so far away. I was so proud that she was loved by so many people.

After her surgery, she was in ICU for 3 weeks and was released right before the Christmas holidays. I called every day, several times a day and the nurse always let me talk to her. The doctor gave her six months to a year to live and said she should just sit back and enjoy life. This was in December of 1997. Over the next few years she defied the laws of medicine and the Mississippi School System. By March of 1998, she was back teaching and in July was given a clean bill of health.

She was an inspiration to everyone. Then, in the summer of 1999, she had more spots appear on her lungs and, this time, had to go through radiation treatments. However, in the fall she was back teaching despite the doctors concerns. She was a trooper and carried on. Her mission was to teach, and she loved teaching with a passion. She touched many, many lives and made a difference for many people.

Together we took on project, a scrapbook of my life. It consisted of all the people in my life for each year and the significant events that happened. As we worked on the book, she reminded me of my clairvoyant youth and asked what happened to all of that. She said, "You used to talk about the angels, and see things. You haven't mentioned it in years, what happened?"

I told her that my grandmother had warned when I was 7 and how it had scared me. I told her that I had been afraid that I was evil, and I told her about my secret life as a healer and a lightworker. I shared about my passions and my desire to make a difference for the world. I shared with her about Indigo Children and about lightworkers and about being clairvoyant and talking to the angels again.

She told me something that I had always suspected but never knew for sure. She told me that not only was she someone who was very clairvoyant, but my grandmother was clairvoyant too. She said she had always known I was more clairvoyant than she was but didn't know how to have me embrace it because it was a taboo subject in my grandmother's household.

As we continued to work on the scrapbook, I got closer to my mother than I ever had been. We laughed, we cried and we connected in ways that I would have never imagined possible. I cherished the moments I got to work on the project with her, learning more about who I am and who she was.

Although she was tired from her battle with cancer, she pushed through and did the things she wanted to do in life. You would never know what she was dealing with and how sick she was by looking at her. She looked healthy and well despite the need for an occasional afternoon nap. However, by Thanksgiving, she had taken a turn for the worse and began having problems again.

She began chemotherapy and had her last treatment one week before Christmas. I spent Christmas with her and I was shocked by the drastic deterioration in her appearance since Thanksgiving. She had lost 30 pounds and was incredibly thin. Over the next several days, between Christmas and New Years, her health declined rapidly.

I knew her time was limited, so my father and I drove over from Alabama on the morning of December 31, 1999 and my father went to say goodbye to her. Despite the rough times after the divorce, by the time of their last meeting they had regained a friendship with each other. I was very blessed. They had worked their differences out when I was younger so there was nothing but affinity and love in their relationship. She grabbed my father's hand and told my father to take care of me. The next morning, I heard her moaning and I went into her room to check on her. She could hardly speak. She held out her hand for me to take it. I grabbed her hand and she squeezed my hand and struggled to get the words "I love you" out. I told her that I loved her and that it was ok for her to go and I would be fine. She squeezed my hand again and took her last breath. I saw the angels peacefully guide her away. She was at peace and she was no longer in pain. I had shared my secrets and there was nothing else to say. I was complete.

My grandmother, her mother, survived her death. I am not sure if my mother had said anything to her about the words she had spoken that had altered my life as a child or not. In April of 2001 I visited my grandmother. She told me she was proud of the connection I had with the spirits and apologized for the words she said when I was younger. It was the beginning of a new life for me as a spiritual being. I was not only now free of my grandmother's past words. I now had her full blessing.

A week later, a ceramic cat that my grandmother had given me fell off the shelf at six am waking me up from a deep sleep. The cat shattered and I knew instantly that my grandmother had passed during the night. I was glad I got to see her before she passed and I was happy that she had realized that I was only out for good of people. I knew that she would be with me forever.

Chapter 8

September 11th, 2001 was a memorable day for all of the world. Not only did I work for a company that had its office in Tower 1 of the World Trade Center, it was also a moment of disbelief and shock for the planet and for me in many ways.

The weekend before that horrific event, my friend Natalie was visiting me in New York. We were out sightseeing and exploring the town and having a great time. We were taking a break and sitting on the plaza by the fountain at the Trade Center, and I suddenly got a horrible pain in my lower back. It was an excruciating pain, and I felt momentarily paralyzed. I had this flash, this premonition of something and I turned to Natalie and I said, "Something is going to happen. I don't know what, but it isn't safe." We walked away, and I didn't think anything about it again.

Something else interesting happened that weekend. My father was also in town on business and was being taken on a dinner cruise around New York. This is something that happens annually and something he always looks forward to. He asked me to be his date for the evening since my step-mother Toni was home taking care of my much younger sister, Kayla, who was not feeling well. I suggested Natalie go to a movie to entertain herself while my Dad and I were on the cruise.

So my father and I went on the cruise and floated right by the World Trade Center. It looked so beautiful with the moon glistening over the Hudson River. It was a picture perfect moment. We took some photos of my father and I in front of both the Statue of Liberty and the World Trade Center. It was a magical night. But I had that same feeling that something was going to happen. I just didn't know what. An intense chill gripped my spine and I couldn't shake it.

On Monday, September 10th, I went to work and left early because my back was bothering me again.

After work, when I got home, I took a hot bath, some Tylenol and went to bed. I woke up on the morning of September 11th

and was in so much pain that I went back to sleep for a bit longer. My boss at the time was in Italy on vacation and I left her a voicemail saying I would be coming in late. I knew she would be checking in and I didn't want her to worry.

Just as I was ready to walk out the door, the phone rang. It was a friend saying the towers had been hit by a plane. Thinking it was a Cessna, I proceeded to leave my house. The phone rang again. It was people calling to see if I was ok. Had I not slept in, I would have been in Tower 1 at the time of impact. I turned on the TV and watched in sheer horror as people began jumping out of the windows, and then the second plane hit. I watched in awe as the towers came crumbling down. I didn't know if any people I worked with were there. I found out later that the people I worked with all had over slept or had train delays except for two. One had just gotten off the elevator and was able to get out and the other was in the lobby. Both were shaken but unharmed. The fact that none of our other staff were there was a miracle.

That morning, I could not find my keys to leave my house. I searched my house high and low and could not find them anywhere. I decided that I was just going to chill and stay put since there was nothing I could do. I found my keys later in the afternoon where I always kept them. I was clear that my mother, grandmother and the angels were with me guiding me and protecting me that day.

I remembered I had the pictures of my father and me from the cruise a few days before. I took the photos to get developed and all of the pictures of the Statue of Liberty came out clearly. The pictures that we had taken of my father and me in front of the World Trade Center did not turn out it all. We had great pictures of my dad and I but no Towers to be seen in the background.

I was emotionally distraught as many people in the world were at this time. I lit white candles, took sea salt baths and drank a lot of wine. I wrote in my journal and drew pictures and ate cupcakes. I watched movies and listened to music. I was fixated by the news and all the stories of 9/11 until I could not watch anymore. It was a day the world would never forget.

That night, I slept on the couch in my living room. I woke up to see spirit upon spirit surrounding me in my apartment. It seemed like there were a thousand spirits or more.

The spirits were all talking to me and wanting me to help. I just burst in tears. I was not sure if I was crying about the spirits being gone and still trapped here, or if I was crying at being overwhelmed by the requests that were being made of me.

I prayed for Arch Angel Michael to help protect me. I got this message, "Dear Child, you are a conduit, and they have come to you to help them to the light. Have no fear, I am protecting you and you are safe." This was great and all, but why me and why now?

Day after day went by and I sat trying to figure out how to help them leave, mainly so I could get some rest. They were in my apartment wall to wall. I saw them day and night, and each day that went by it seemed that more and more of them found their way to my apartment. I lit a sage stick, which clears a space of intruding energies, and waved it corner to corner in my apartment. But it didn't really help. I still wasn't sleeping well. I had so much activity in my apartment, I could not take it anymore. I felt like I was a prisoner in my own home. It was intense. I felt like I had to be polite to these intruders in my house. I was a wreck. Zoe, my cat, was restless. It wasn't fair.

Finally after about five days, it finally dawned on me what I needed to do. I had to write a prayer for all of them to go to the light. I must have lit 10 white candles, and that night, as I was going to sleep, I asked the angels to help them with their transition and move them toward the light. I called on Arch Angel Azrael and asked him to help the people move to the light and to comfort the loved ones they had left behind.

As I drifted to sleep for what seemed like the first night in days, I was visited by an Indian Spirit Guide, named White Buffalo Moon. He looked to be about a million years old with long, silvery braids and an amazing headdress bursting with colorful feathers. I had never encountered him before and was intrigued by him and, also, hopeful he could help me.

He showed me this desert with a river running through it. He grabbed my hands, looked me in the eyes and then slowly moved our hands above our head. It reminded me of the tunnel you make when you play London Bridge as a child. White Buffalo Moon started chanting in a language I had never heard. I just listened in awe not knowing what I was supposed to do. Then he said very powerfully and in a demanding tone, "All spirits, go to the light. You are safe. You are protected. Please leave this woman's side. You have loved ones waiting for you on the other side."

Then there was a pause. Suddenly, one by one, the spirits went through our "London Bridge Tunnel" and stepped into the water to purify themselves. They then slowly went toward a bright, peaceful light on the other side of the water. As the spirits were going through us, I felt safe and surrounded by light. One by one they disappeared until they were all gone. I began to cry as I felt the releasing of the energy around me.

White Buffalo Moon looked at me and said, "My job is done with you for now, I will return when you are ready for the next step in your training." I was thinking, "My training for what?" White Buffalo Moon smiled and looked at me as if he were reading my mind. He squeezed my hands and said, "Do not worry. You will know when the time comes. I will be guiding you. Know that you bring light. You are a lightworker who is here to heal. You have a gift and are guided by many angels and guides. We are here to support you. Go now my child and rest. There is a new day coming." Then he faded away. I woke up the next morning, with an enormous sense of peace around me.

Chapter 9

Over the next few weeks, I spent my days working from home, and I spent my nights saying prayers and lighting candles to help any other spirit who may have been left behind and suddenly appeared to be helped to cross over. I was not thrilled with the sudden idea of being a conduit and a medium. Did that mean that I was going to see dead people all the time? I suddenly felt like the kid in the movie, *"The Sixth Sense."* This is not what I signed up for.

Arch Angel Michael kept telling me to go to the World Trade Center site and I kept saying "NO, I don't want to." Well arguing with an angel is kind of useless since they don't give up. I have learned over the years, when you get that strong of a message, just do it. So about two weeks after 9/11, I went to the World Trade Center not knowing why I was going or what I was going to do there. But I trusted Arch Angel Michael and knew that something amazing would come of it.

I walked around the ground zero site and didn't say anything to anyone. I just stood there in awe looking at the destroyed store fronts bordering ground zero. Then I heard a voice say, "Send energy." So I just stood there and sent energy to whoever needed it. I felt this enormous amount of energy escaping me, and at the same time I felt this enormous amount of energy moving through me. I didn't know who exactly I was sending it to but I was clear that someone or many someones were receiving it. It just kept flowing and flowing and flowing for what seemed like an eternity. Then I heard, "Sit and just close your eyes. Imagine all the people there are healed. Imagine all the fear and tears being gone. Imagine that they are at peace over the loved ones they have lost." So I did. By this point I figured it was pointless to argue or ask why. I just listened and did what I was told.

As I sat there, I noticed that it began to get silent around me. People had stopped weeping and sobbing and there was peace. People began laughing and the dense energy was subsiding. Silently, I smiled as I knew why I had come. I was there to bring peace to people even without them knowing it. I thanked the angels for the push and after a few moments gathered my things and left.

As I passed by police officers and firemen who looked bleary eyed and as if they had not rested in days, I thanked them for everything they had done. Many grown men started to shed tears in the acknowledgement of themselves and their brothers and sisters they had lost.

It was an eye-opening experience for me, that I could bring peace just by intention. I began to wonder what else I could bring by using my intention.

It was also a great lesson in shielding myself. Like many people, I am empathetic and sensitive to energy and can absorb negative energy around me if I am not careful. Being empathetic means that you absorb the energy around you and you think and have the experience that they are your feelings, thoughts and emotions. I realized that being empathetic has both great and not so great aspects. If you are aware that you are an empathetic person and pick up the emotions of people around you easily, shielding yourself is a great way to live without fear of emotions you may absorb from others. If you are not aware that you are empathetic, shielding gives you a temporary sense of peace.

I went home, took a sea salt bath, which I do often to release excess energy, thanked the angels for the day and went to bed. This new-found mission was wiping me out.

Chapter 10

Over the next few months I was able to experience my clairvoyance and my intuitiveness at a new level. I saw spirits and released them. I received messages from loved ones, and I was able to use it to heal people around me. It seemed constant, and it got easier and easier to deal with the more it came up. I still had the questions, "Why me? Why was I the one? Why now?" The angels only answered, "Because it is in preparation for bigger things to come." I didn't understand nor did I care to. I guess it was part of my mission and was to be figured out at another time. Angels don't work in "human" time. They work in their own time. So what may seem like eons to me, is a blink of an eye to them. So I knew more information would be needed and given when the timing was right.

Patience is not one of my strongest suits. In fact, on the patience scale, I am a 0. I want something and I want it now. I don't often like to wait for things; however, the angels kept reminding me to have patience. Good things come to those who wait right? I know, I know, everything would come to me, but when? I wanted to know what the angels had in store for me, and I wanted to know now. At that point in my life I was clearly in for a change, but in what direction?

So I read as much as I could and gathered as much information as I could and studied what I had learned. I knew that I would be using all my knowledge later in life to create new ideas and adventures, but in what arena, I didn't know. For now, I was to be a student and learn, absorb, create and grow.

Chapter 11

That year was a long and trying year for me. I had lost my Mom the year before, my grandmother in early 2001 and then September 11th. I was all stressed out and nowhere to go.

My father decided to have the family take a vacation out of the country for Christmas. My father travels quite a bit and was very high up in the frequent flier awards and booked us all on a trip to Germany and Austria. I was thrilled to get out of the hubbub of NYC and go to some place far, far away.

We spent Christmas snowboarding in Austria. This was definitely my sister Kayla's idea. Kayla loved the idea of being a snowboarder. I, on the other hand, being someone who hates the cold weather and who has never ever skied, was nervous about snowboarding. I was excited about the trip with my family but less than thrilled at spending the day on the slopes and out in the cold. Every morning at 5 am we would rise and shine, have breakfast and hit the slopes for lessons.

Kayla actually got quite good at snowboarding. I, on the other hand, looked forward to having lunch every day. I had spaghetti every single day we were there. Strangely enough, the German food is one of my favorites, but I craved the pasta and meat sauce. Believe it or not, the spaghetti was some of the best I had ever tasted. Maybe it was because I was so cold or maybe it was because I was hungry. Who knows, who cares. I looked forward to it every day.

After our adventures on the slopes, we spent some time traveling through other areas of Germany and Austria.

We took a day trip to one of the World War II concentration camps, Dachau, in Bavaria. It was the single most eerie and uncomfortable place I had set foot in my life. The cold, dreary day only compounded the experience of entering the dingy, grey gas chambers where 190,591 people had been exterminated.

Walking through the camp sent chills down my spine. I could hardly imagine what it was like to have been there. To this day, thoughts of it still chill me. I just remember the sights, sounds and smells as if I had been there myself during those horrible years. There was an intensity to the energy that I had not experienced even at the World Trade Center site. It was a fierce and powerful energy that was full of sadness and grief. There was also so much anger and fear in this place. I could feel it penetrating deep into my bones, despite the energetic shielding I had done repeatedly while I was there. I knew somehow, even though it was painful, I needed to experience this energetically.

It was a haunting experience that aroused in me enormous compassion and gratitude. It left me with compassion for the people and souls who were exterminated as well as those who survived and gratitude that I did not experience it personally. My few hours there were enough for me to get a sense of what it must have been like. But it also reminded me how lucky we are, that no matter what evil persists in the world, we have the strength to overcome it. No matter what life hands us, we have the power and ability to move beyond it. I had no idea how much that would ring true many times later on in life.

Chapter 12

Upon returning to work after my trip to Germany, it became clear to me that I needed to do something to connect to my spiritual side again. I had really let that part of me slide. I did a little work here and there but I had stopped doing the research and studying that I loved to do. What mostly occurred were brief moments of calling on the angels when I needed something.

Quite a while had passed since my powerful encounters had happened around the World Trade Center. I could not believe that it had been almost a year since 9/11. I had really let my connections slip and was starting to long for that connection again. The incredible work required to not only rebuild our physical office, but also the business in a tough environment, left me stressed and miserable. I woke up feeling ill all the time, and I was clear I wasn't doing what I wanted to do. The messages I kept getting were to leave this job that I had loved and go do something else. The pressure built and I was getting to a point of ongoing frustration. It was too much. I finally listened to the persistent guidance I was receiving and left my job. I didn't have another job lined up so I decided to take some much needed time to relax, rest and explore who I am.

I began to meditate more and explore the power of quieting the mind. I saw enormous value in this as our mind chatter is never-ending. I often called on Arch Angel Jophiel to work with me and help clear my thoughts and bring clarity. She is the angel of Beauty and Grace and works to de-clutter things both in the physical space as well as our minds. I was also compelled to do yoga more frequently, receive light healing more, and as a result started to get more and more comfortable in my own skin. All of this was very soothing and natural for me and also very healing. The more I did it, the more information I received. As I continued to open up, more and more experiences started happening which then left me with the next thing to deal with. So it was an ever- expanding process for me. One day I would be confident and flourishing in life, and the next day I would be confused and unsure of my direction.

As I was trying to find the "something else" I was supposed to do with my life, I did temporary office work. This "temporary" work lasted several years. It was a very blank part of my life. No excitement, no fulfillment, and I was definitely not making the difference I was called to make. It was the exact opposite of why I had left my previous job. I felt trapped in my body, my mind, my spirit and was very uncomfortable. No one at these offices I temped at was on a spiritual journey, so I felt I really couldn't talk about such things in these offices. It was almost like I was back in my teenage years, except this time I did not have my Mom here in the physical realm to talk to.

Work, work, work … the corporate field was not for me. But I lived in New York City and needed money to play and to pay the bills. The way I saw it, until I figured out what I wanted to do with my life, or until the angels told me what to do, I could tolerate my current situation. I was wrong. The more I denied the angels and my clairvoyant abilities, the more I was miserable and suffered. This went on for a while.

It was 2003, and I had been working my butt off. I decided I really needed a vacation, really badly. I didn't know why but I had this sudden calling to go to Greece and the Mediterranean. I was obsessed with going and surrendering to the obsession seemed like the only way to resolve it all. I began researching and studying the culture and asked the angels to help me find a way to go. I didn't know why but I knew I had to be there. Now.

Chapter 13

I think I was a travel agent, and a pretty darn good one, in a past life because I always seem to find great travel deals at random places. This time I found three weeks in the Mediterranean for a price that was what I would consider really cheap. It was a trip of a lifetime. I would spend some time in

Spain, Nice, Greece, Rome, Pompeii, Capri among others and even a stop at the famed casino in Monte Carlo. It was more than I had asked for and I was so excited. Thank you, Angels! They had come through for me once again. Four weeks later, I was packed for the trip to the Mediterranean and ready for the adventure of my life.

I knew this journey would be powerful in many ways for me, perhaps historically, artistically, culturally and spiritually. So I came prepared for all of it. I went by myself intentionally so I did not have to adhere to anyone's schedule. I like to do the things that I want to do and this trip was about me regaining who I am and about me waking up from the stupor I had fallen into.

I took my journal, a sketch pad, crystals and my vision. I knew something big was going to happen to me on this journey. Would I meet the love of my life? Would I find my passion?

The trip started off with three days of sightseeing in Barcelona. I was fascinated by the beauty of the city and the generosity of the people. I don't speak a word of Spanish so I was grateful that the majority of the people I met spoke English. Barcelona was stunningly beautiful. It reminded me of a cross between San Francisco and New Orleans.

I toured the old town and was astonished at the amazing structures and buildings created by the avant garde, Spanish architect, Gaudi. He soon became my favorite artist/designer to look at in Spain. I bought a book about him to bring back. His work was such an intriguing part of the journey. I loved this art nouveau fantasy and wanted to experience more. I went to the House of Gaudi, a museum that held collections of his work. Just being in the environment designed by this innovative genius, pushed me into my own creative vortex. Energy around me began to swirl. I saw beautiful swirls of purple, green, blue and pink light circling in patterns around me. I knew the angels were with me and they were evoking a creative energy in me that had been suppressed. I had not drawn anything in a long time. I had sketched some stuff in the past few years but nothing worthwhile. But suddenly, I had this massive desire to draw and recreate some of Gaudi's masterpieces. I sat in the park overlooking the Mediterranean Sea, drawing a mosaic iguana that was designed by the famed artist. I disappeared into another world. I imagined myself as an artist, alone, on the Mediterranean Sea, drawing pictures to feed me and stay alive. It seemed a very familiar moment to me, as if I had been there and done that before. Perhaps it was a past life moment creeping in. Whatever it was, it was very powerful. I was so immersed in my drawing and the vision, that I must have fallen asleep. I woke up about an hour later with my head in my sketchbook and the pencils by my side.

I have always loved and had an appreciation for art. However, my love for the artistic world grew as I explored the Picasso Museum, the Spanish Museum and the house of Gaudi, a museum of all of Gaudi's masterpieces. I was intrigued in the Egyptian section of the Spanish Museum. Something about the artwork of Egypt being in Spain baffled me but I enjoyed it regardless. In the Picasso Museum, I explored the haunting paintings of Picasso's early days and the abstract paintings of his later years. The energy in the museum was palpable and very distinct. It wasn't an energy I had picked up before. I could feel Picasso's deep gaze as I engaged in the paintings and I knew he was watching me. I was the only one in the museum, so it was like Picasso and I were having an intimate moment to ourselves. I walked around marveling at the work and trusting the energy that surrounded it.

It was eerie and mind-blowing to be in the house of Picasso with all of his works. Picasso has always been one of my favorite artists and I have always admired his work. There is so much complexity and so much passion in his work and so much story to be told. I prefer abstract art over conventional art pretty much like I prefer the abstract life in comparison to the conventional life.

I wanted to learn more, and I asked the angels to guide me. I felt Arch Angel Gabriel's energy around me, and I heard her say things to me about the paintings I was looking at. She helped me see things in the paintings I had never seen before. I saw images in the paintings that are painted subliminally telling a message. There is a ton of sacred geometry in his works, a deep connection to spirit and a passion for love and understanding. I had a new-found appreciation for the master of the abstract art and his work.

The most powerful connection in Barcelona was at the La Sagrada Famiglia Cathedral. This Cathedral took my breath away. It was designed by Gaudi and is considered one of Barcelona's most prized treasures. Gaudi unfortunately died before this magnificent piece of work was completed. This Cathedral is stunningly beautiful and powerful, and it exudes spirituality and a Divine Connection in every way. You hear of music or art being channeled. This Cathedral was clearly channeled by the famed Gaudi from some higher vision.

Each angel that was carved on the side of the building came to life and told its own unique story. I stared wide-eyed as these images came to life and listened to what they had to say. I was getting an incredible amount of information from the angels about the church and about my mission on this trip. The carved angels were all beautiful and I could hear and see the love that was poured into each artistic piece. The spirit energy was profound, and there was a warm of angels in and around the cathedral. There were green, purple, yellow and blue lights swirling and moving around the cathedral as if to protect it but also to create a powerful Divine Connection for anyone who was interested in absorbing that connection. I felt as if the angels were just saying, "Surrender. All is well." The peace that I felt was very strong and overwhelming. I felt like I was being wrapped in a giant blanket and given a huge hug. Tears streamed down my face as I let the angels in. I knew they were working on me and healing me in many ways. I just sat and let them guide me. I felt so much energy and pain from the past being released. After a few moments, I felt like a new person with an enormous sense of peace. Maybe this moment, this exact one, was why I had made this journey.

Chapter 14

The next part of my trip was sailing to Nice, France. Nice is just beautiful and looked like it was right out of a painting of the French Riveria. The scent of the rich and sweet lavender fields filled the air with a lovely fragrance. Beauty surrounded me everywhere I looked. I could have sat there with my feet dangling in the water all day and daydreamed. I was so content and I felt so mellow enjoying the luscious life on the Riviera. I could see me living the life of a princess and vacationing or having a summer house there and sitting in a café' on the Riviera watching the people go by.

Later in the day after I had seen all I wanted to see in Nice, I took a bus to Eze, an ancient medieval village built into the side of a mountain. Eze had many spirits around it. There were a variety of tree spirits, fairies and human spirits flitting and floating around. As I walked through the crooked cobblestone streets, I had a brief experience of what life was like in this time period. This structure was said to be around in the fourth century, the time of the Phoenicians. The castle and the ancient ruins hinted at stories of times long gone by. I saw pirates climbing the mountain to do a sneak attack on Eze. I felt as if I were intruding into another world. I noticed I was tired so I went to look at the water. What a view I had! It was very grounding as I sat and took pictures of the Mediterranean Sea looking up at me from below. While it was a haunting experience, it was peaceful at the same time.

The village of Eze had been turned into a tourist haven with many souvenir shops offering a variety of things from local artisans. I visited a perfumery that makes delicious, sweet-smelling perfume from local flowers, including jasmine and lavender, two of my favorite scents. While I did manage to escape the persistent beckoning of the storekeepers, I did not manage to escape the sweet-smelling perfume. I walked out of the perfumery with bags of some of the best smelling perfume I have ever found. Every time I wear it, I still find it captivating and reminiscent of my time in Eze.

My next stop was the amazing palace of Monaco. Monaco has to be one of the most beautiful and charming places I have ever seen and by far the cleanest. It reminded me of the times I had walked through Disneyland and been present to how pristine it was -- the moment something fell, it was magically whisked up by an "invisible" person whose only job was to make sure there was never trash on the ground. I immediately considered becoming a citizen, but much to my dismay, I discovered that you have to be born there or marry someone who is a resident to live there -- and the prince was already taken. Bummer!

Chapter 15

As I walked around the village near the palace of Monaco, I immersed myself in the beauty that surrounded me and was completely in my own world. I visited Princess Grace's grave and saw where her children lived.

I was near the palace in the shopping area, listening to music on my Ipod, when the next thing I knew, I was tumbling down one of the numerous flights of marbled stairs that dot the village. I sat up gathered my thoughts and realized I could not move. I was afraid that my ankle was broken. I thought, "Oh My God, this is supposed to be the vacation of my life and I cannot move." I started screaming for help but I don't speak French and given I was in an alley in Monaco, I didn't think anyone would hear me. I began to panic. I seemed to be stuck at the palace of Monaco, which isn't necessarily a bad thing, but if I was going to move in, there were definitely some aspects of my life I would need to handle before taking up residence in an alley none-the-less.

So, I took a deep breath and had the angels send someone to find me. Luckily, within minutes, a couple who spoke English stumbled upon me and helped me up. Thank you angels! The man, whom I will call Steve, rushed to the bus driver to tell him what had happened so the sightseeing bus I was travelling on that day would not leave me behind. The woman, whom I will call Carol, helped me slowly walk to the bus. I was in so much pain, I thought I would pass out with every step. All I could think of was "Why is this happening?" Even though they sent someone to find me, I was pissed at the angels. I was having fun and really enjoying myself for the first time in a long time, and now I had to deal with THIS! Even though I was mad, I figured that the angels had a reason for my fall and would let me know in due time. It took a lot for me to really just let my anger go. It was definitely supposed to be another way.

I never saw Steve and Carol again but was grateful that the angels, once again, had answered my prayers and sent someone to my rescue.

I was on the bus on the way to the famed Casino in Monte Carlo, trying not to cry and hide the disappointment that was there. However, I was so excited about being in a place I'd heard so much about, that I figured that even my throbbing ankle was not going to keep me from enjoying the casino. After all, I'd be sitting down, having a few drinks and playing the slots. Not a chance!

As soon as I stepped off the bus and put pressure on my foot, I shrieked and collapsed in agony. There was absolutely no way I was going to be able to stand, much less walk into the casino. So I sat on the bus, by myself, in a dark garage, in Monte Carlo, and cried.

I cried long, deep sobbing tears. It was a mixture of pain and of shame. Here I was in one of the most famous areas in the world and I was sitting in the dark by myself while the other people from the bus were having fun. It wasn't fair! I was in so much pain from the fall, and I was so embarrassed and mad that I had to miss out. I was mad at myself, the angels and everyone else I could think of. If I was suffering, everyone else should, too.

Someone was kind enough to bring me some ice so I could put my leg up and ice it. I had a lot of time to contemplate what was happening and a lot of time to have the swelling get bigger. I sent energy haphazardly to my foot without any intention. I was still mad at the angels for having me fall, be in pain and miss out on an exciting time. I had a box of raisins in my purse. That was the only food I had with me, so I ate the raisins and took a Tylenol and went to sleep. I had dreams of the angels giving me specific messages about my healing and about what work I was to be doing. I knew Arch Angel Raphael was there and that he was taking care of me.

I was in a deep stupor and awakened a few hours later when everyone returned to the bus, excited about their winnings and sad about their losses. It was time to get me medical attention since my ankle was the size of Montana and as many colors as a big box of Crayola Crayons. I knew I had to do something. So I did what I do best, put my hands on my foot and allowed whatever healing energy I could muster to come through. I felt Arch Angel Raphael guiding me but I was still pissed. This was "supposed" to be the best vacation of my life. I was still trying to figure out what the heck the angels wanted me to learn.

I got to the doctor's office and it was determined that I had a level-5 sprain, interior and exterior on both sides of my ankle. Great, Great and Double Great! I didn't even know what that meant, but it didn't sound good.

What it did mean was that I was supposed to keep it immobile and was not to put any pressure on it whatsoever for the next TWO months. WHAT! I was in a foreign country and couldn't put any pressure on my foot. What was I supposed to do, sit in my hotel room and watch bad movies? I sat there in disbelief and really wanted a way to get back at the angels. How could this happen? But I knew, if I was going to have any kind of fun over the next three weeks, I had better suck it up and let the angels guide me and heal me. I took a deep breath and surrendered.

It took a lot to just surrender because I was not a happy tourist camper. This was _not_ how I wanted my much needed and well deserved vacation to go. When I got back to my room, there were a dozen roses, chocolate covered strawberries and champagne. The card read "We are so sorry to hear about your incident. If there is anything you need, let us know how we can be of service. Please do not hesitate to ask". It was signed by the managers of the hotel, Michael and Raphael. I could imagine Arch Angels Michael and Raphael sitting there with a big grin on their faces and I had to laugh. If that wasn't confirmation that the angels were with me despite my anger, I didn't know what would be. So I called the front desk and had them get some Epsom salt and a pack of ice, took a hot bath and went to bed. It had been a long day, physically and emotionally and I was ready to hit the hay. I was in excruciating pain and took the medicine the doctor had given for pain in hopes that it would help me sleep better. All the time I was asking the angels to heal me and to make the pain go away.

Chapter 16

The next morning, we sailed to Italy. We spent an entire day at sea so I had plenty of time to rest my foot and my spirit. The water was stunning, such a vibrant shade of blue and so serene and peaceful, and I just stared into the vast blue ocean daydreaming as we passed by. Since this was both a land and sea vacation and I was by myself, I never had any place to be except for the meals, and the pool area. What a life I was living right now! I was sailing on the Mediterranean Sea, being waited on hand and foot until I could barely stand it, which took a really really long time.

I was given a wheel chair and an escort to the dining room, and I soon became the talk of the town, the woman who fell down the stairs at the Palace of Monaco. I felt famous. People came up to me and offered service in any way I needed. People offered to get food and bring it to me and to help me to the pool. I was first embarrassed but then became a free spirit, enjoying myself being pampered. Maybe this was part of the angel's plan to force me to have interactions with people and spend less time by myself. I had been completely content listening to my music, drawing and reading; but now people kept talking to me, making me connect with them, something I had often avoided in my life.

The next day after breakfast, I was scheduled to travel to Florence with a short stop to see the Leaning Tower of Pisa. I was excited but had no idea how I would be able to wheel myself around. I was afraid I would be left behind. A young man named Hans had offered to push me around Florence in the wheel chair. I was grateful and inspired by his generous offer. I learned a lot about him, about who he was and his life. He was from Finland, on a research tour of the Mediterranean, was married and had a little girl who was four. Well, even though he wasn't available for me to date or create a romantic relationship with, he was fun, generous, and great to look at.

Hans and I became fast friends. He wheeled me around the cobblestone streets of Florence through the exquisite scenery that surrounded us. He thought it was fun to pretend I was a speed racer from the cartoon and he ran and wheeled me around fast and furious. We laughed until we cried. I bought him a traditional Italian lunch to thank him for being so kind and I knew that this was all part of the angels' plan. Maybe the accident needed to happen for me to "lighten up" and have fun and not be so immersed in my own world.

As we approached the statue of David, I stared in disbelief. This was probably one of the single, most beautiful, stunning pieces of art I had ever seen. The pictures we see of David are beautiful but in no way match the beauty of this sculpture when seen in person. As we journeyed through the Italian city, I felt the presence of the many great Italian artists.

Michelangelo's presence was very strong as we marveled at his many masterpieces that were on display. Like my moments with Picasso, I was able to connect and feel the presence of the master. I didn't communicate but I did notice a warm, loving individual who was very immersed in and very proud of his art. The beauty of the city was also mixed with the beauty of the ancient life. Every cathedral had its story as did every piece of artwork. Each artist was there showing pride of their pieces and wanting to be seen. I felt like I was in a battle of the artists type phenomenon. Each one wanting and arguing that their art was the best. It made me laugh to see such a vision.

Later that day as we visited the Tower of Pisa, I was overcome with a sense of peace, love and calmness. I was also in awe of how this giant structure so visibly leans over and has not simply collapsed. It really leans. I managed to get a picture like most tourists do of me attempting to hold it up. It came out quite funny given I was in a wheel chair and holding up a tower was quite an accomplishment. It had been a fun and magical day, and I was exhausted from the enormous amount of sightseeing we had done. As in Spain, I had a much bigger appreciation for Italian art and culture now that I had experienced it firsthand. I just loved Italy…the food, the people, the culture, art and history…all wrapped into one beautiful package!.

I went back to my room and looked at my purchases from the day. I love jewelry and always manage to find a beautiful piece of jewelry wherever I am to remind me of my travels. I bought a beautiful Italian gold bracelet in Florence that sparkled like the top of the Chrysler Building in New York. I took some time to draw and write in my journal before I went to bed. My drawing was becoming a daily part of my trip. I felt like it was a release of some sort and at the same time it opened up my creative channels. I wrote in my journal about the day and about the things I was seeing. I was clear there was something big for me to learn on this journey, and this was just the beginning. I turned on the TV to relax, and as I drifted off to sleep, I heard, Arch Angel Michael say, "Trust my child. This is part of the journey to discover who you are and who you will become. We are guiding you. You have the ability to heal. You are healing yourself at many levels on this trip, emotionally, physically and spiritually. You are releasing old patterns, discovering new ones and learning to trust yourself. This time is for you to learn, to love and to be loved. Do not discount anything on this trip. This journey will re-ignite a part of you that has been lost and release a spirit that has been trapped. Do not fear, it will make sense soon. Now, rest; tomorrow is a big day for you."

Chapter 17

I was awakened in the morning with the sunlight shining in my room. I stretched and looked at my ankle. No change. I took a deep breath and realized my hopes were a fantasy. The doctor said two months and it had been two days. The next part of the journey took me to Rome where there is enough history, art and culture to last a life time or two. I began the first of a few days at the Vatican. As I was being wheeled around from art to art I got overwhelmed with the talent that was expressed by the artists. I was amazed at the art in the Sistine Chapel and the Vatican City Museum. I shuddered as I could see the art and hear the story. Rome has a lot of pain and a lot of power attached to it. Even though I was in one of the most holy of places, there were areas that had an intense, uncomfortable energy. I asked Arch Angel Michael to shield me from this energy so that I could allow myself to be engulfed by the amazing, creative presence.

As we were leaving the Vatican, the Pope (John Paul II) was making his way across the plaza. We made brief eye contact and he paused for a second to nod at me as if to bless me. I was so honored I began to cry. These were tears of hope and of joy. Even though I am not religious, and have never really been, I have a huge respect for the Pope. I felt like the angels guided me to have my injury so I could have this happen. I felt this enormous energy run through me and run through my leg. It was very powerful. I knew all would be ok. When the pope passed a few years later, I had a moment of reflection on my brief but powerful connection with him.

When we arrived at the Coliseum, Hans wheeled me around and I saw visions of many gladiators engaged in battle on the field. I had to do a double take, but they were still there. I could see the armor, the swords, and I could feel the intense action. In real life the gigantic structure lived up to every photo I had ever seen. It was powerful, beautiful and haunting. I just let the visions come and the visions go. I knew this deeper view I was getting was all part of my clairvoyance but it was still overwhelming. I had Hans take me to a nearby park where we had a nice Italian gelato for a snack.

It was a very emotional day. I was tired and ready to go to bed and it was early. As I fell asleep for the night, I envisioned my ankle healing and I surrounded myself with Arch Angel Raphael's powerful and healing green light. I could feel it deeply penetrating my ankle and my entire body for that matter. I felt like I had absorbed a lot of intense energy from the day, so I asked Arch Angel Michael to remove it. I took a few deep breaths and felt the heavy energy leave my body and my energetic field and I felt relaxed. I knew that I needed to rejuvenate myself because the next day I was going to Greece and that something exciting awaited me there.

Chapter 18

I was so excited we were finally getting to Greece, I couldn't sleep. I sat up in my bed wide awake at 5 am, ready for the world. My tour to Athens began at 11 am so I had a few hours to kill before we left for the tour. I didn't want to go back to sleep, and it was too early for breakfast. I knew that today was special. I could feel it in every ounce of my being. I didn't know why but I could not wait for the tour to begin.

I knew that I could not be wheeled up to top of the Acropolis because of the many stairs, and yet I also knew that, without question, I had to reach the Parthenon. This was a moment I had been waiting for my whole life. I felt the power of the Greek gods waiting for me and I had to be there to experience it fully. There was nothing that was going to deter me from going. Nothing! I had been fascinated by the Greek gods since I was a kid and this was as close as I was going to get to experience their power first hand.

I took a deep breath, asked Arch Angel Raphael to help me, and I wheeled myself out to the pool. I knew what I needed to do. I had sprained my ankles many times before and my mother's remedy had always been to do movements in water to stretch and strengthen my ankle. As much as I wanted to stay in bed, I also wanted to walk up the Acropolis. So I went for it.

The sun was just starting to rise and there was no one around. Good, I had the whole pool to myself.

I managed to somehow get out of the wheel chair, and scooted to the edge of the pool. I stuck my foot in the chilly waters only to pull it back out in an instant. I slowly put it back in the cold morning waters and I circled my foot about twenty times to the right and then circled it about twenty times to the left. I took a deep breath and then did it again and again and again. The pain was intense and I just wanted to give in and cry. I called out to the angels, "Angels, please help!" I took a moment, took a deep breath and circled my foot in both directions once again. Then, when I had a little movement going, I outlined the letters of the alphabet with my foot a few times to create movement in all directions. It was getting easier and less painful every time I did it. I repeated this cycle of movements a few more times and began to get a glimmer of hope that, maybe, just maybe, if I did this long enough, I would be able to walk up the Acropolis. It seemed like a long shot but one I had to go for.

After a while of writing the alphabet with my foot, I felt like I could do more. I eased myself into the pool and held onto the side and kicked my feet and legs to get a different muscle working. I had been sitting in a wheelchair for several days, and I knew my muscles were a bit weak. I did this very slowly and gently and eventually progressed to a much more vigorous movement. Then the final test came. I went up and down the ladder, up and down the ladder and up and down the ladder. I took a breath and went up and down again several more times. I looked at my watch and it was 9:15 am. I had been doing this for over three hours. I really didn't want to risk overdoing things and decided it might be best to stop and get ready for breakfast.

As I slowly climbed out of the pool, I was able to stand and put a little weight on my foot. I cried tears of joy. I didn't want to push it, however, so I wheeled myself back to my room, took a hot Epsom salt bath and went to breakfast. I felt like I had this wonderful little secret and could not wait to show Hans my little miracle. He really had become a close friend and good travel buddy on this trip. I knew he would be happy for me and excited for himself that he didn't have to try to push me up the stairs at the Acropolis.

After breakfast, I went to my room, and even though the doctors had said it would be a month minimum before I could even think about being able to use them, I grabbed the crutches I had been given. I put my arms in the arm guards, grabbed my camera and proceeded to take baby steps to the lobby where I was meeting Hans. I paused after a few steps to rest. I could feel my ankle throbbing but I was determined to have this work. If I needed to slow down, I would. But this was going one way. MINE!

Hans was waiting for me already when I got there. He was as shocked as I was by the improvement. Even though I was walking with the crutches, he insisted that we put the wheelchair in the bus. JUST IN CASE. After arguing for a few minutes, I reluctantly obliged.

Chapter 19

I was very excited. We were in Greece! I could feel it was going to be a magical day. As we drove around the historical city of Athens, I was filled with glee. I had done something that the doctors said was not possible. It had only been 6 days and I had defied the medical world. Outside I was calm, cool and collected. Inside I was jumping up and down and thanking the angels. I had forgiven them for the fall, and I knew that they were at work to help me uncover things I had never known about myself. I knew my healing powers were intact and that this was the first step in really healing myself and being able to heal others.

We drove by the Olympic Stadium that hosted the first Olympic Games (which was being remodeled for the 2004 games) and the Theatre of Dionysus, (the first theatre), among many other famous sites. I was here! I was really here. The Olympic Stadium was exactly how I pictured it would be with athletes playing to win a medal for their country. I wondered if there was any way I could come back in a year for the Olympics. It was going to be a stretch but maybe... after all Anything is possible! I was so excited, I couldn't see straight. I could not wait to get off the bus. I was tugging on Han's sleeve and letting my excitement run wild. "Look at everything. Look, there is Mt Olympus." The excitement built.

We got to the foot of the Acropolis. I looked up at the Parthenon that awaited me and I could feel the rush of energy surrounding it and me. I could feel the energy of the goddesses Athena, Aphrodite and Hera encircling me. I was tingling with anticipation. I took a deep breath and began climbing the million stairs of the Acropolis, and with each step got more and more excited and got more and more tired.

I looked up at the sky and was not happy to see that it was getting dark with rain clouds. This was not a good thing since I was on crutches, and I feared that any rain water would make the stairs and ground slippery. Han's begged me to turn around, but I knew that I had to get to the top. When I set my mind to something, there is nothing I can't accomplish.

A bolt of lightening struck in the far distance and I could hear the thunder rumbling. I asked the angels to hold off the rain until I was done. Once again they came through. Thank you Angels. With all the dark clouds and rumbling thunder, I had a vision of what it was like many thousands of years ago when similar storms thundered through ancient Athens. It was as if Zeus were speaking.

Slowly I climbed the steps and wondered if I had made a mistake. My ankle throbbed and I was really tired. I still had many more steps to go. Should I turn around? I heard Arch Angel Raphael say, "You can do this. Keep going. You are doing great." It was all I needed to hear. I proceed to the top of the Acropolis and put my arms up in the air. It felt like such a victorious moment.

I took a few moments to just be with myself. I went to the edge of the hill and sat down not only because I needed to rest, but also because I wanted to absorb the energy that was surrounding me. I looked over the city, the harbor and the many wonderful and historical sites that Athens has to offer. I closed my eyes and allowed my mind to just wander. Within moments, I felt Athena and Aphrodite's goddess energy around me. It was magical. I relaxed and absorbed their powerful energy. It was as if their energy was surrounding me, and I could feel giant arms around me. I was very comforted. I felt my breathing get lighter, I felt my energy rise, and I felt my fears disappearing. I basked in that energy for a few moments, absorbing all I could. Somehow, I knew I would be back in Greece and that everything would be ok.

After my short but exhilarating rest, I walked through the temples and took a moment to sit in each one, meditate and relax. I asked for guidance as to what my life was for.

Athena came through loud and clear and said, "bringing wisdom to the world." Hmm, I liked the sound of that. I thought it would have been great to have more information but I would take what I had gotten for now. Maybe she was referring to the school I had always wanted to open. I relished each moment at the Acropolis and Parthenon and seeing the beautiful statues that were paying homage to the gods of the Greeks. I sat with Athena's message and remembered the words Arch Angel Michael had spoken to me the other day, "Do not discount anything." Words cannot truly express the complete enjoyment and sheer excitement I had experienced. I felt a great sense of power and a great sense of peace. I was content.

I also knew that my life would not be complete until I visited and sat in the Theatre of Dionysus. Given that so much of my life had been devoted to acting and performing, I knew I had to be where it all began.

I had Hans help me down the stairs and over the cobblestones to the amphitheatre. I sat in the amphitheatre on a bench that must have been thousands of years old and wrote in my journal. The amphitheatre was badly in need of restoration.

Many of the benches were broken or crumbled. The stage still had some original pillars and structures and I was amazed at the fact that they were still standing.

After taking a few pictures of the great theatre, I closed my eyes and had visions of the Greeks performing their famed comedies and tragedies. I saw flashes of scenes from *Antigone* and *Oedipus the King* and I also saw a moment of Socrates' *Lysistrata.* I felt as if it were being performed just for me. It was great to see the costumes and the flair and the intensity of the actors. It was so amazing to see how the performances were played out. I was so immersed in that other world that I did not hear Hans' repeated calls. He was tugging on my sleeves, calling my name and I obviously did not want to be interrupted. I was too much enjoying a moment of theatre history that had been a part of me in this lifetime -- and perhaps other lifetimes.

Hans finally pulled me away from the theatre to hit the Palatka, the shopping district of Athens. Shopping! Whoo hoo! I did spend some time perusing the stores, mostly to find they all offered about the same merchandise. I bought a few small things that would remind me of my journey to Athens and then sat down to lunch with Hans for a traditional gyro sandwich and baklava. It was delicious and I savored every bite. It had been an incredible time in Athens and I was satisfied. I was still relishing the moments on the Acropolis and Athena's words of wisdom! I couldn't wait to find a payphone to call my friend Cathy back in New York and share about the experience at the Acropolis and with the goddesses. She had said she knew something incredible had to happen, and it had.

I knew that my being here was a completion of my past and a learning of who I am and what I am meant to do. There were things I needed to trust, to let go of, to observe, to heal and to see with new eyes. This trip was about me regaining who I am. I now see that the angels had supported me in the healing after my accident as a way to experience the Divine Glory that I felt that day atop the mountain, overlooking the Greek city with so many stories and so much history. It was also a lesson in trusting my own power and ability as a healer and really ensuring anything is possible when you put your mind to it and have the angels by your side.

Chapter 20

I had plenty of time to reflect on what I had learned thus far on this trip. I sat by the pool, read, drew and wrote in my journal. I was so glad I had come on this trip, and I still had about 10 days left! We were off to Mykonos and Santorini next.

Santorini…….Aghhhhh! Need I say more. As soon as I saw it, I felt nauseous and dizzy and, at the same time, excitement filled me. Santorini is one of the places where Atlantis was said to be located, although the heart of it was said to be in Thira, the north end of the island. I was speechless as I stared at the beautiful view that was in front of me. I felt like I was in paradise.

I looked up at the mountainside that lie before me and felt the enormous heat from the volcano. The heat also built inside me. I could feel all the Atlantean energy tingling in my body. I had decided this was a day just for me. I really needed to bask in the energy of Atlantis and reconnect with that energy. Hans went on a motorcycle tour through the island and I took my drawing pad and my journal and explored the island's energy.

The only way to get up to the summit of the volcano was either by donkey or by cable car. The donkey sounded fun and I thought it would be interesting to ride it up the mountain like you see in the movies that are shot in Greece. Now mind you, I had never even ridden a horse, except a wooden one on a carousel, and I asked myself, "How hard could it be?" Boy was I in for a surprise.

I was placed on my donkey sidesaddle, and we were set free to go up the mountain. I had my crutches dangling from the side. I had no guide like you see in the movies, just me and the donkey doing its thing going up the mountain. The donkey decided running would be much more fun and, despite my screams of terror, he did not slow down. The Greek men laughed as this funny American woman rode the donkey to the top of the mountain. I was so glad to get off the raging beast and decided right then and there that, without question, the cable car was the on*ly* way to make the return trip.

When I got to the top, I gasped. The beauty of Santorini was unquestionably breathtaking. I looked over the whitewashed houses to the crystal blue water of the sea. I could envision the beauty of the island many years ago, perhaps even in the Atlantean times. I felt like I was in another world. Maybe I was.

I sat there daydreaming about Atlantis and this overwhelming sadness crept up on me. It took something for me to let the emotions up as I do not like to cry in public. Although I had done it many times on this journey, this time, I just let it out. I sat there and sobbed for what seemed like days, but in reality was only a few moments. I just let the tears stream and the emotions flow. After a few minutes, I had so much love and energy present I was overwhelmed.

I saw a vision of the Atlantean times that I had seen many times before. This time the vision was very intense. I saw the giant crystal generator with the lasers of energy beaming from corner to corner in a magnificent temple. I could see the marble pillars and the beautiful marble stairs that surrounded the generator. I could feel the heat and energy running through my body and my ankle. I could see the magnificent blue waters and watched longingly as the beautiful dolphins that swam in it. I so longed to go back there to that time. I felt dizzy and displaced and the nausea grew. What was happening? I just let it be for a moment, and then I looked down to find a small crystal quartz laying at my feet and choked back a laugh. I put it in my pocket thinking this was definitely a sign for me and definitely a sign from above that all was well.

I ventured over to the natural springs, sat on the edge of the spring and put my injured foot in the warm waters. The springs were heated from the volcano which now lay dormant. The water was soothing to my tired, aching body and it felt like a gift from the gods for my sore ankle. I had such an overwhelming sense of peace and an overwhelming sense of healing. I knew that this was only the first of many trips I would make to Santorini. I knew that it was only a matter of time before I did more work with and connected to the Atlantean energy. I knew that Santorini would be a place of research, connection and discovery in the future.

While enormous healing took place and a huge energetic release happened, I knew that I needed some time to rest and to process it. I was so overwhelmed by the energy of the Island that I had to get off the island, for now. I made my way to the cable cars and rode down the mountain. I watched the donkeys making their way down the mountain, and I was so happy I was not on top of a donkey for my downward journey. The cable car was a much more peaceful and relaxing ride. Thank you, angels.

I went down the mountain, back to the boat and sat with my feet dangling in the swimming pool for a while. I daydreamed about the dolphins, and sipped some frozen fruity drinks, watched the sun set and then went to my room to relax. I took a hot bath and went to bed. It had been a long day filled with adventure, excitement and energetic release; but a long day nonetheless.

Little did I know when I booked this trip that I would grow spiritually as much as I had. Looking back, I was not the same person that had boarded the plane to Barcelona a short time before. I was opening up to my spirituality and my healing abilities in ways I could not have imagined happening back in New York. I had a new found sense of peace and a new found sense of myself. All the pain and stress of 9/11 and of my mother dying had disappeared. This trip had given me the much needed opportunity to really look objectively at how much I love experiencing the mystical world. I was getting excited about life again and what I could use it for. I began to realize I wasn't stuck with anything. The accident and trusting the angels to take care of me was a real test of my willingness to surrender to powers bigger than myself. My impatience was challenged by the angels who always wanted me to trust them. I had to keep giving up my desire to make everything happen now. Taken all together, I did not feel like and was not my old self anymore.

Chapter 21

Our next stop was a return to Italy and this time we explored Sorrento, Napoli, Capri and Pompeii. I was getting pretty good at getting around with my crutches. In Capri, I was mesmerized again by the crystal blue waters that surrounded the island. There was just something about it that always seemed to take me to another world. While I definitely enjoyed the shopping there, I much more enjoyed the times to myself and the times where I could create, dream, visualize and remember. This to me was so much more interesting.

I went to the Blue Grotto and sat there having visions of mermaids playing and splashing in and around the coves that were there. I could envision them sitting on the rocks, swimming and laughing with the dolphins and fish and bringing joy and magic to the worlds around them. It was such a fantasy. Or was it? I loved connecting with the mermaids and the fish in the Blue Grotto. It gave me a sense of peace and a sense of wonder. It was like a dream or a fairytale. I could have spent the whole day there immersed in the energy and the magical wonders of the ocean, but I felt that since I had come all this way, I should see other parts of the island as well. So I ventured out and explored the Isle of Capri. I noticed all the Gucci and Cartier stores and the beautiful gardens surrounding them. Although, the entire island was beautiful, I still most loved the Blue Grotto and my mermaid and dolphin friends.

Next, I travelled to the historical city of Pompeii to see its ancient ruins. As you may already know, when Mt. Vesuvius erupted, the people of Pompeii were frozen in time by the hot lava and ash which buried the city. They were forgotten for 17 centuries until archaeologists began excavating the city in the 1750's.

Pompeii was exquisite, a truly historic site. As I walked through the hallowed halls, I could feel and see the sprits as they walked passed me. I could see the agony in which they suffered. I could hear their screams and I could see their pain.

It was quite a remarkable and intense experience. I could see the remains that were frozen in the ash. I could see the original paintings that were unscathed and I could see the beauty in which this city had once existed.

I loved Pompeii. As I hobbled through the streets, I got a glimpse of how the royals lived. I particularly remember one villa, its art and the beautiful tiles that covered the floor. It looked as if it had been built just recently. Everything was intact and had been restored beautifully. I walked out to the gardens and just sat there for a while engaging myself in thoughts of what it must have been like to be here, living your life and then have it end in a second. There was nowhere to run and what could a person do? As I gazed at Mt. Vesuvius, I thought how strange a place the world is. The more I sit and listen, the more I learn. It is funny how it all works out. There is so much out there to be told, all we have to do is listen.

The world is also very peaceful. The oceans are calming as are the mountains. The thing that I see interrupts that peace is man and the language and morality he brings to it.

I was at the end of my trip and there was a part of me that was sad. I wasn't ready for it to end. I looked back over my pictures, drawings and journal. I had created new worlds and new experiences in the three weeks of my journey and grown exponentially in the process.

I looked at all the purchases I had made, the people I had connected with and the stories I had to tell. I looked at the pictures I had taken and I reminisced over all the amazing things I had seen. I looked at the ways I grew spiritually, mentally and emotionally. I let people take care of me, I experienced new and old cultures and, as I reflected on it all, it seemed to me almost as a dream.

Hans and I had breakfast together the last morning. It was great befriending him and sharing this journey. He had been a good person to spend time with. I wished him well on his research and journey. He had been the perfect angel sent to me for this journey.

Chapter 22

When I got back to New York, I was a different human being. I had accomplished a lot on this trip and was humbled by the world I had experienced and opened myself up to. Like many people, my Mediterranean adventures began to seem like a distant memory that was not quite real. I had to look at the pictures, drawings and journal to snap myself back to the fact that I really had been to all these amazing places.

Immediately, it was back to work for me. I had had fun and played hard but now, back to reality. I was leading a workshop that started a few days after I had gotten back. I could see that my trip had really impacted my leading and my speaking; I really was not the same person. Over the next few years, my life of working with the spiritual world was pretty consistent. I spoke to the angels daily, played with crystals and used them around me, and shared with friends about my experiences. This was getting to be a part of my everyday life. Almost daily, my friends were asking me what the angels were saying, which angels were around them, and did I have any messages from their deceased loved ones.

I was still holding back somewhat though. It was still tough to be completely open after all the teasing I had experienced as a child. There were still things I had not shared, and I was uncertain the degree to which I could share them. In fact, many of the details in this book are being told in depth for the very first time. The angels became a "normal" part of my life and I felt that people were beginning to finally understand me.

A lot of it began with me accepting myself. It took me knowing and accepting I am a powerful lightworker and healer. The burdens of the past had started to lift and I was having fun again. The Mediterranean trip had been an affirmation of my connection to the world of spirits and gave me confidence in the role I could play in the future.

People began asking me for healings and readings, and I trusted the guidance I was receiving about it. I had been having a lot of fun in my life and that was a big release for me. I no longer felt alone, scared or apprehensive about who I am or what I know.

In 2004, I went back to work for the company I had left in 2002 but in a different department. I decided I needed structure in my life and the office temping had not been providing stability. I had loved the company I had worked for before and the training I had gotten. The past two years had allowed me to recover from stress of rebuilding the department and the general mood of the world after 9/11. I was now ready to jump back in to a full-time job.

I took a different position, one that had me interact with lots of people and make a difference for them daily. I began to flourish and excel in all areas of my life. I was leading workshops and seminars that were making a difference. I was accepting myself as a spiritual being, and I was playing bigger games than I had been playing earlier in my life. Life was moving with velocity.

Chapter 23

Things went really well for a year or so until 2005 when I was diagnosed with melanoma in my lower right leg. I had gotten to a place of pure light and was being a powerful lightworker in my life. So what happened next was enough to test me in every possible way.

The very first hint of the melanoma showed up in the summer of 2004. I was vacationing at Disneyworld and discovered this weird, ugly, flesh-colored, mole-like growth on my right shin. It looked like someone had super glued a pencil eraser on my leg. I played around with it some but didn't really think anything about it.

During the summer of 2005, I was taking a mini-vacation from work. I was wearing short, flirty skirts and showing off my tanned legs. The growth was there and I wanted it removed. It was an ugly distraction to the legs I was working so hard to show off. During my regular visits to my general practitioner he had never expressed any concern about the mole, nor had my dermatologist. So why should I be concerned?

A concern for vanity, not health, kicked in, and I decided that I wanted the growth gone. So, I went back to the dermatologist to have it removed, and he said "if you want to have it taken off, no problem. We can remove it. But no need to worry, it is just a mole."

But it wasn't. Two days later while I was at work I got a call that no one wants to get – the unexpected call that no one can ever be prepared for. Up until then, I had been a healthy, happy woman who loved to go to the beach, dance and wear short skirts. The next words on the phone altered my life forever. "We're sorry to tell you this. You have an extremely rare case of melanoma and need to have emergency surgery now." I remember sitting at my desk in total shock and thinking, "I am going to die." In a pretty frantic state, I walked over to my manger's desk. She was having a phone conversation so I sat numbly waiting for her to complete the call. As soon as she hung up the phone, I broke into tears. I told her that I had just gotten a call from the doctor and that I had melanoma that needed to be surgically removed immediately. I just sobbed. Margot, a co-worker, who recently completed a 30-year nursing career, assured me that everything was going to be ok. Little by little other people I worked with came to see if I was ok. I was so scared. After a few moments of consoling words, I went to a separate office to call my family, my friends and schedule a doctor's appointment to meet with the surgeon. As I sat down to make these calls, I thought that this was one of the few times where being vain about my appearance had paid off.

I spoke to several friends and the more I spoke to them, the easier it got to talk without crying. The hard part was calling my Dad. After all, he had already lost his ex-wife, my Mother, to lung cancer in 2000. Even though they had been divorced for many years, they were still close, and it had been hard on him when she died. So, naturally, I did not want to give him bad news about me. I didn't know how he would take it. As I gave him the news, he was actually very calm, cool and collected. If he was upset, he never let me see it. When I talked to him, I poured out my heart and was relieved that he handled the news so well. I told him that I would call him after I had had the meeting with the surgeon the next day. The last call I made was to the NYC Cancer Institute to set up the appointment for the next morning.

I remained at work and kind of stumbled through the rest of the day. Later, I made a few calls to find someone to go with me to my appointment the next day. I knew I could not do this by myself. A wonderful friend named Mary said she would come with me to my appointment to meet the surgeon. Mary is always so peaceful and so great to be around. I had so much anxiety, emotion and nervousness in my usually calm and centered body. I was glad Mary was going with me.

That night, I could not sleep. Millions of thoughts were racing through my mind. Am I going to die? I am so young. How could this be happening to me? I have so much going for me. I want to make a difference, am I going to be able to do that? The questions went on non-stop. I was doing well in my job and was getting ready for a promotion. Was this all going to end? Was I going to lose my job? It was a completely restless night. I asked the angels to help me. Their grace was the only thing that gave me peace that night.

Early the next morning, I met Mary outside the New York Cancer Institute. When we were finally brought in to see the surgeon, we were met with such warmth, compassion and love, that I knew I was going to be ok. He explained the surgery in detail. I was extremely happy to hear it would be an outpatient surgery. He told me that I would be sore for a bit until I healed. He explained to us that the tumor was a very rare type of melanoma and occurred in less than 1% of melanoma cases. The tumor was actually underneath the skin but had broken through causing the raised nodule.

He would have to make an incision on my right ankle and would cut the tumor out including a circular area around the tumor to ensure it was all gone. I would have to take a few days off from work to recover, and depending on how the surgery went, we would decide whether chemo or radiation were needed. Well, that was good news. His gentle, loving way brought lightness to the entire situation.

Mary and I really liked the doctor. He was compassionate and seemed like he really cared about me and my healing. We decided that he should definitely be the one to do the surgery. I looked at my schedule and we decided to do the surgery the following Friday, about a week away. That would give me the weekend to recover. We made calls to people that we needed to call: my father, Glenn a doctor friend of ours and other people who were waiting to hear the results of the exam. I had a week to get things handled at work and in my life. I also had a whole week to deal with my mind.

During that first visit to the doctor, the nurse handed me some pamphlets about melanoma to review. Reading them was like reading a self-fulfilling death prophecy. After reading the first three sentences, I just knew I was going to die. It said melanoma was the highest killer of Caucasian women between the ages of 35 and 50 in the world. 100,000 people died in NYC alone in the last few years. Blah, Blah, Blah……….. I was petrified. I called Kristi, an amazingly powerful woman who was also a coach/mentor in my life. While pamphlets like this, I am sure, are intended to comfort people by providing useful information, the world they create is one of fear and dread. If you take the case that what you think or speak creates the world you live in, these pamphlets are a dreadful reminder that you are not well and they instill the fear of death in you before you even know what is happening in your life. I recommend that anyone suffering from any disease, first give the pamphlet to a friend or family member to read so they can evaluate the worth and spirit of the information.

Fortunately, Kristi told me to immediately throw the pamphlets in the garbage and get them out of my house. She then told me to go boil some tea and then take a hot bubble bath. She stayed on the phone with me until the wee hours of the morning, calming me, soothing me, helping me relax so I could sleep, and assuring me that everything was going to ok. It was one of the most profound experiences I had ever had. I didn't know a human being could care so much. She made herself available to me throughout the week, and boy, did I take advantage of it!

So many people stepped up to support me. Many people called even though, at times, they didn't know what to say. People came by to see what I needed. My friend Tony, who subsequently became my housemate, said he would stay at my house and take care of my pride and joy, my princess cat Zoe. People offered to come to my office and volunteer so that the work would still get done while I was out. People all over the world put me on prayer request and healing chains. I felt like there were many beings on earth and in the spirit world helping me.

I think it is very important to have many people around whenever people are dealing with important circumstances like this. There is something very powerful in creating a world where you are not dealing with something alone. Those people force you to relate to the world rather than be obsessed by what's going on in your head.

I had been connecting with the angels again for a while now through visions, hearing and sensing them. This time when I asked them to help me, I kept hearing, "Have faith. It will all work out." This was a message I had heard many times before and I had learned to trust it. As the surgery got closer, I began calling on the angels more and more. I kept getting that same message. Given the angels had never steered me wrong, I trusted their message which gave me hope and light.

Chapter 24

My father flew into New York the night before my surgery and stayed at a hotel near LaGuardia airport. He arrived about 6 am at my apartment the morning of my surgery to pick me up. We took a cab to the hospital and on the way stopped at a deli - my Dad needed something to eat. I watched my father enjoy his coffee and eggs and bacon breakfast. Gosh it smelled good! I was on strict instructions to eat nothing before breakfast.

Mary was meeting us at the hospital. She was going to be with us for the first part of the morning – really to be more with my Dad than with me. I knew her calming presence would make it easier for my Dad. I had people set up in shifts to come and be with my father and be with me when I woke up. Mary, Gaby and Christine were all set up to be there. They are all very powerful women who would bring a sense of peace, light, and laughter to the situation.

We arrived at the hospital and I checked in. I promptly was wheeled to the lab where I was having the pre-op procedures. I was to be injected with blue radioactive dye. Fun! This dye shows the surgeon where the melanoma is located and if it has spread to the lymph-nodes or another location. After the lab tests, I had a big problem trying to get around the hospital -- my new radioactivity kept setting off the hospital security alarms! Every time I would go by an alarm, it would go off and I would have to explain over and over that I had no fire alarms or bombs. This did not help the already fragile condition of my nerves.

After all the pre-op procedures, I spent a lot of time waiting in the waiting room. I was now wearing a blue hospital gown, those hospital socks with the treads on the bottom and paper shoes. I was a sight to see and I was stylin'! I looked around the waiting room and realized how silly I must look in this getup, and I laughed. Maybe it was my nervousness, maybe it was my way of calming myself, but I just let the laughter out. It felt so incredibly good to laugh. It was the first time I had laughed out loud in a long time. I did not even care what anyone thought.

After waiting for what seemed like an eternity, I was finally asked to come in and meet with the doctors. Mary and my Dad came in to join us for the conversation. As I handed them my jewelry, my watch, my earrings and my belly-button ring, the fear set in again. Giving up my personal belongings really left me feeling naked and alone. This was really happening! I tried to be brave, but I really wanted to cry. Mary and my Dad both hugged me and said they would see me in a few hours.

The doctor led me into the operating room. It seemed really weird to me to walk myself into the operating room and climb up on the table. It was almost as if I were saying, "Here I am! Cut me open and do what you will with me."

The anesthesiologist was rather charming. He offered me an apple martini for "happy hour". 10, 9, 8, 7………. and I was gone.

The next thing I knew I was looking around and trying to figure out where I was. I have a faint memory of the breathing tube being yanked out of my throat and gasping for air. I wanted some orange juice, or something since I had not eaten in days. Well hours, but it seemed liked days. A nurse brought a cracker and some orange juice - big mistake. It made me nauseous the moment I swallowed it.

My Dad and Gaby had walked into the recovery room to see me. Mary had left and Gaby had arrived while I was in surgery. By that time, I was in so much pain that Gaby asked the nurse to give me something to relieve it. The pain pill put me back to sleep for another hour or two. I assumed it had been a long and trying wait for my Dad and Gaby.

Finally I woke up again and my Dad and Gaby were right there, and this time, I was able to keep some juice down. The surgeon had said the procedure had gone really well and he was pleased. He was releasing me. Hooray!!! I was very ready to get out of there.

Since I lived in Queens, one of New York's outer boroughs, my father had booked a room for us at a Marriott near Grand

Central. This made it easier for him to take care of me as well as to provide a much more convenient place for my Manhattan-based friends to come visit.

So my Dad, Gaby and I got into a cab and headed toward the Marriott. The pain meds were starting to wear off and I could tell that this was going to be a long night. My father had checked into the hotel room and gotten my prescriptions filled while I was in surgery, so we were able to go straight up to the room. I lay in the plush, soft covers of the bed and watched bad afternoon TV, really wanting food. Cupcakes, chocolate, ice cream, hamburger anything. I was starving. Bring it on, baby! Give me everything you got!!

When Christine got there, Gaby left. My Dad decided it was a good time to go out and get something for me to eat since Christine was there with me. He went out and brought back CHICKEN BROTH! Was I ever disappointed! A hamburger, french fries and large chocolate shake really sounded good, but he and Christine convinced me that broth would probably be best. Hmmmmm. It was a tough sale but I ate it anyway.

Around 6:30 in the evening Christine left so I could get some rest. It was so great to have her there, but it had been a long day and I was ready to just be quiet and alone.

The next day people called and people visited, bringing yummy things to eat - ice cream, fresh fruit and cake. YAY! Finally, people were reading my mind.

I watched movies with people; I received flowers; and I had tons of calls and cards. I felt so loved and taken care of - like a princess – for three days. I was getting spoiled. Then, my father had to travel back to Alabama where he lives. Tony, my friend who was house and cat sitting, came to get me at the hotel and we took a cab back to my fifth floor walkup in Queens.

It was not fun trying to get up the four flights of stairs to get to the fifth floor. In fact, it was just downright brutal. After two flights, I just sat down in the stairwell and cried. My leg and groin area hurt so badly from the effort of taking the stairs that I felt nauseous. Why didn't I live in an elevator building? I begged the angels to help relieve this pain. I could not go one more step. It was at that moment I realized I wasn't going to be doing anything for the next few days other than resting and healing myself.

I was supposed to work the next morning and I just could not see it happening. Right there sitting in the stairwell, I called my friend Chris, who was managing our office. I asked him to tell everyone who needed to know that I was not coming in to the office and that I would have to take it one day at a time. I finally made it up the stairs, onto the couch, and curled up with my beautiful tabby cat, Zoe.

She was so happy to see me and just loved me as much as she could muster. Her purrs made my tears go away and her kisses made me smile. She was an angel being sent to have me heal with velocity.

Chapter 25

After a few days of resting, I decided to attempt to go to work. I could not get shoes on, yet I was determined to go. I had one of those socks with the foot treads on my foot and prayed that that sufficed. It took me 30 minutes to walk to the subway that was only two blocks away. What was I thinking???!!!! By the time I got to work, I was so tired and irritable; I was ready to go home. What a journey it was just to get there.

After working a few days, I decided I had made a big mistake by going back to work and was not ready. So I took four more days off and rested, slept and healed and learned to love myself during this period. I learned that I needed to listen to my body, listen to the angels and take care of myself.

I did a lot of healing work on myself.   Of course I communicated and listened to the angels and their guidance. Every night I envisioned Arch Angel Raphael, the angel of healing, and his green light bathing my leg. I envisioned the light pouring into my leg and my leg absorbing it like a sponge. I carried crystals with me. Crystals have natural healing properties that you can access simply by holding them or placing them on your body where healing is desired. Crystals can also be charged and programmed to heal and bring in specific kinds of energy. I employed my skill as a Reiki master. Another healing method I used is called Vortex Healing. It is a divine healing modality that brings several different types of light to heal, nurture, and get at deep, core issues.

I also had many conversations with the people in my life which provided opportunities for sharing, healing and love. And lastly, I watched tons of movies in between the much needed resting and sleeping.

After a few days, I was well-rested and went back to work. It still took something to climb four flights of stairs, walk three blocks, climb the stairs to the subway, ride the subway, climb the stairs out of the subway station, and walk to the office. However, it was all worth it, just to get out of the house. What a relief!

After two weeks, it was time for me to change my bandages, and I nearly fainted at the sight of my leg. It looked like it belonged to Frankenstein's monster. It was very skinny from atrophy and had a multicolor phenomenon of black, blue and green with about 24 stitches in it. I had never seen anything like it, except maybe on TV. But this was my leg! It wasn't supposed to look like this. I have a strong stomach but this made even me a bit nauseous.

I took it slowly and dealt with the shock of my leg looking as badly as it did. It looked like I would have a massive scar. Fear took over and I cried. I braced myself, took a few deep breaths, and began to apply the antibiotic cream the doctor had prescribed. I just couldn't stand to touch my skin! It felt like leather. It didn't seem like me. I asked Tony to apply the cream and put the clean bandages on for me. He graciously agreed. I closed my eyes and just let him do it. As Tony was doing this, I looked up to the ceiling, really to the sky, to the angels and said, "Please heal me fast. I don't want to have to keep doing this."

It was now approaching September. I continued to go to work but kept my leg up in a chair. I allowed people to run errands for me which is a big deal because I always want to do everything myself. And, lastly, because my leg and foot were so swollen, I wore fuzzy slippers in the office. Someone had loaned me black, fuzzy house slippers and I wore them with pride, looking like Norma Desmond in *Sunset Boulevard*.

The swelling was tremendous. My once shapely leg was now a giant club foot. The only way I could look good was to put the short skirts in the back of the closet and get out the long skirts and pants. Just as I was having to change my wardrobe, I was definitely altering many ways in which I dealt with my life.

I had learned a lot while dealing with cancer. I learned to allow people to contribute to me, I learned to trust and have faith at a whole new level and I learned to be grateful for what I had. I learned that the angels were always by my side -- angels, both in the spirit realm and the physical realm who came to my rescue over and over and over.

I started paying more attention to my interests, and I began noticing a drastic shift in what I held as important. My once wild and partying days were gone. I was definitely looking toward living a life of peace. I started noticing colors, bright, beautiful, glorious colors around me again. I hadn't really been present to the richness of life around me for a while. I felt like a kid in a candy store. Lights were getting brighter, music was getting clearer and peace was beginning to prevail around me.

The reawakening I had been longing for was beginning. I was reconnecting to the spirit world. Something that had been a part of me since childhood was returning fully. All my moments in Greece and Italy, the impact of September 11th and all the other experiences were all a foundation. I felt invigorated, enlivened and excited! Through my intention to heal myself, I had regained my connection. I was determined never to lose it again.

Chapter 26

It took a while for me to regain my sense of self after my first battle with cancer. I felt as if a part of me had died, and, in fact, it had. While I had one tumor removed, it seemed like a chunk was missing not only from my leg but also from my spirit. The uncertainty caused by the changes I was going through left me feeling as if I didn't know who I was. Weeks after the surgery, I tried to be positive and keep a positive outlook.

I knew that keeping a positive outlook and a positive attitude were critical, and I did whatever I could to maintain it. It took a lot of energy to stay positive during this period. However, I was tired all the time, really, really tired. Part of me wanted to just rest and part of me felt I should be doing something. I was used to being very active, but I also realized that allowing myself to rest was an essential part of the healing process.

I kept hearing the word "Trust." Trust what? The answer was always the same. "Trust. All is well. You know the answer, listen to your heart."

This was a message I had heard over and over throughout my life. However, every time I received that message I had this surrendering that I had to go through. I always expected an answer to be given to me and it never was. No matter how many times I heard the message, I always had a moment of confusion and frustration because I wanted to know exactly what the angels were talking about, and I wanted to know Now. But angels don't work in "now" time.

All there was to do, at that moment, was to focus on my healing and getting well. I sent energy. I sent healing. I asked for energy. I asked for healing.

As the time passed, I got stronger physically, mentally, emotionally and spiritually.

I had to go to the doctor every two months for check-ups. I had to get a complete body scan from head to toe that searched for any new tumors, bumps or lesions.

The first couple of exams found me free from any new cancers. This was good news! Then, there was one of those moments that stopped my beating heart. I had an "unusual" looking spot on my back that needed to be looked at more closely. Panic set in.

It turned out to be a small abnormal mole that was benign. Thank you, angels! The doctor wanted to remove it to keep it from becoming a problem in the future.

Chapter 27

By May of 2006, I had progressed to going to the doctor from every two months to every four months. By December 2006, and a continued clean report, I didn't have to return for an exam for six months. I felt like the angels were on my side rooting for me and pushing me forward.

I was really progressing in my job. I was getting everything set up to interview for a bigger position. A position that would have me travel, make a difference and help humanity. I had studied, been trained and prepared for it for a long time. I was very excited and very nervous at the same time. This was a big deal for me and I was turning myself inside out to have it happen.

While I was focusing intensely on this career advancement, I unknowingly, again, began to forget about the creative and spiritual aspects of my life. This, after I had promised myself I would never do that again. Fortunately, I was able to distinguish that I was not paying any attention to these areas and how it was beginning to wear on me. I was hiding and was not expressing my connection to the angels freely. All the work I had done to uncover, heal and gain power in my healing and clairvoyant capacities seemed wasted. I had to face the fact that I didn't know how to pursue this very demanding job and stay actively engaged in my spiritual life. My job used the logical part of my mind, the spiritual used the creative part. I didn't know how to merge the two together.

Chapter 28

I pretty much felt lost without the angels there to guide me. It wasn't like they went anywhere, I just couldn't hear them. Sometimes that happens. I get too much in my logical brain and I forget to connect with my spiritual side. At the time, It felt like they had stopped talking to me, but I now know what was true is that I wasn't listening for or to them. They were always with me every step of the way.

I didn't feel that I was receiving clear guidance. I was confused and felt alone. Meanwhile, things around me were moving with velocity.

A year had passed since my surgery and I was in a totally different place in my life. I was experiencing myself as a powerful leader in ways that I had not ever imagined possible. I was very focused on my career. .All the years of training, studying, conference call after conference call and development had paid off and I was beginning the interview process for a major leadership position with the company.

As I began to look closely at this new, potential promotion, it looked really good on paper. I would make a profound difference in the world. I would travel the world. I would be a part of a powerful group of people. I would get a decent salary increase. It was everything I had been working and training for.

And yet, as I really took in the magnitude of the position, I began to doubt whether I was capable of it. This would vastly alter my life and my lifestyle! And, while I was getting excited about it, I was having second thoughts. Why was I so nervous when this was what I had thought I wanted?

I noticed that I missed feeling involved in real creativity. I began thinking of how I missed talking to the angels and doing my artwork. I wondered if I would really enjoy being on the road most of the time. Who would take care of my cat? What about my apartment? I didn't want to give up either.

I really felt torn. I asked the angels for guidance but I did not hear a response. Then, in October of 2006, the moment I had been waiting for came. I had a series of interviews scheduled that would determine whether I would be promoted into this new position. I was excited and at the same time really scared.

Unfortunately, on my third and final interview all of the fear and uncertainty got a hold of me. I just froze up and the interview didn't go the way I had hoped. I did not move to the next level of interviews, and I was devastated. I choked up and sobbed to the point where I could hardly breathe. I sat stunned and in disbelief as I took a cab back to my house. I had been so excited before this interview. I didn't know how I could face the people I worked with who were all eager to hear what they assumed would be a great outcome.

I was angry, pissed off, embarrassed and confused. I was mad at the angels - again. I had worked so hard for this so why didn't the angels help me achieve it. Why?

I couldn't gather my thoughts enough to answer that question. I sat in bed sobbing and not knowing who I could call. It was 1 am and most people I knew were in bed. Besides, I was in a state of shock and was upset. I knew that if I did talk to someone, I wouldn't make any sense. Needless to say, I didn't sleep well. My mind ran through the conversation over and over. I totally messed up. I felt sorry for myself, blamed myself and blamed everyone else. I just wanted to pack up and move away – far, far away -- to a place where no one knew me, and I didn't have to face anyone.

It took every ounce of courage I had to go to work the next day. I knew people would be curiously waiting to hear what had happened, and I just didn't want to speak. I left a message for my boss, and when he got there, he pulled me into his office so I could speak. It was the first time I could even attempt to speak about it. I sobbed and he just sat and listened.

Chapter 29

It took a lot of healing for me to get over that one, more than even Reiki could handle. I kept hearing the angels say "trust" over and over again. I knew there was something for me to see that I had not seen before, but I was not sure what. I had conversations with people, did everything I could to have my broken heart mended. My life was on a different path now and I was not sure what that path would be. My future was now thrown into question. I felt lost and I felt like I didn't even have my angels to guide me.

I really had to deal with myself and my emotions. I was still so angry and so hurt, and every bit of confidence had gone out the window. I was mad at myself. I didn't know who I was, what I was here for and what I was supposed to be doing. All I wanted to do was escape it all by sleeping.

The job I had once loved and once thrived in was suddenly not moving me forward. I had lost my bearings and I my faith in what I was doing. I had a lot of questions and no answers.

I asked the question, "Why angels? Why are you ignoring me?" And I heard this voice say, loud and clear, "My Child, we are not and have never ignored you. You could not and would not listen. Since you have free will, we cannot intervene. But know that we have been guiding you. All the training you have received and all the time and effort you have put toward this is not lost. For now, heal yourself. Forgive. Let go of the resentment and know that the training and the learning and the passion will lead to new things. As one door closes, another will open." This was the first time in what seemed like months that I heard my angels. I sat on my bed and let the tears stream until I fell sound asleep. It was the first good sleep I had had in a long time.

Chapter 30

Every day I went to work and every day I wasn't sure why I was staying there. If I wasn't going to get this particular promotion, I wasn't sure if I was really interested in staying. However, I was suffering, the people around me were suffering and there was no bright light to lead the way. The once bright light was now a dark and dingy cloud.

I decided that if I wasn't going to get the career advancement I wanted, I would, fill my life with things I wanted to do. I began to put the fun and adventure back in my life. I went skydiving, I began sculpting and drawing again and I went back and studied Reiki. It had been 20 years since I had been declared a master, and although I used it all the time, I wanted a greater sense of clarity about exactly what I was doing when I did Reiki. It was a much different and deeper experience than the one I had had at 14. This time, I really could get my hands around it.

I studied it again and got a deeper understanding of the ancient Japanese healing. I began releasing a lot of pain both, physical and emotional. I knew this was just what I needed to be doing. In learning, I was healing myself and acquiring new ways of moving energy that I had not known before. Shortly thereafter, I was declared a Reiki Master again.

Six months after that failed interview, my boss presented me with a choice - to continue to work there or not, but I had to decide. Clearly I had not been happy and he had sensed that. This was a job I had loved, thrived in and had even produced great results in. If I wanted to continue to work there, fine and if I wanted to resign, fine. Either way it was my choice. My boss said that he had a particular desire that I stay, but ultimately, he wanted me to be happy and the choice was mine. To force the issue he gave me until 6 pm that day to make my decision.

I did not get any work done that day as I agonized over what I should or should not do. I hadn't been truly myself and happy in about six months. I had had some moments of glitter but mostly I was creating a self-induced world of gloom. It wasn't the job or the company, I just saw that it wasn't myself expression. I am clear it was me. I am an artist who wanted to create and this just didn't fit.

During this time I had befriended an amazing woman, Nancy, who is now one of my best friends. I spent what seemed like hours that day on the phone with her trying to figure out what to do. I also saw my friend Mary and spoke with her. No one could or would give me the answer or tell me what to do. It was my choice.

As I sat there weeping at my desk for the whole world to see, I felt this enormous pain in the top of my head. All of a sudden my head felt as if someone had rammed a giant cylinder or tube through my head. I felt all this energy pour in to me. In that moment, it felt like my crown chakra had exploded and I was downloading all of this information. But what was the information? I heard the angels speaking in what felt like a negotiation of some sorts. It felt as if they were negotiating what was next for me. I began to wonder why this negotiating hurt so badly. I was experiencing the most horrific pain and given that I was not getting any work done anyways, I decided to take a walk and get some food. Maybe that would create a space of clarity.

I went for my walk and the message I got was that I needed to heal people. DUH, I know that. This was not news to me. "Choose Heather," I told myself. Just choose. Why are you suffering? AAAGHHHH I could not see straight and I could not choose. "Angels, help! Give me a sign. What do I do?"

When I got back to my desk I had pretty much decided that my days there were numbered, and the best thing for me to do was to move on. But, I was terrified to say something. I received a call that made a huge difference for me in the moments leading up to my final decision. It was someone acknowledging me for making a huge difference for them. In that moment, I changed my mind. I chose to stay in my job that I had loved so much and chose to make a difference. In that moment I also had chosen to make the angels a permanent part of my life again. I knew I need them and that I cannot fulfill my purpose without them and their help.

I began producing good results again. Not as good as prior months, but I had turned around a lot of the work I had destroyed in my moments of self pity. The department was going well again. Two weeks later I was offered the position of being manager of the department. I thought this was my opportunity to create new things. I was thrilled and jumped at the chance despite the amount of work it entailed.

Chapter 31

During this time of my life, my friendship with Nancy bloomed. She was the first person I told about the promotion. I had known Nancy for about 3 or 4 years. During the brief times we ran into each other, I had always liked her, but nothing had ever developed further in our friendship. But then we took on a project together and during that time we connected and became fast friends.

The first time she came to visit me in New York for a girl's weekend (she lives in Connecticut, a few hours away), we connected at a very deep level. I began sharing with her about the angels. I related how they had been a part of my life, that I could see myself doing some more work with them, and that I wasn't sure exactly how that would show up in my life. I felt guided to tell her all of this and somehow I knew she would understand. That weekend I introduced her to crystals, angels and Turkish food. We shared, discovered a lot about each other and laughed 'til we cried. I didn't remember laughing that hard in a long time. It was an instant bonding, and I felt that I had not only gained a new friend, but a sister as well.

I also discovered that she was profoundly clairvoyant and was a healer in her own way. Untapped and completely natural, she began to have prophetic visions and began channeling before my eyes. She began talking about an orange light around me. She saw visions of me being in Lisbon and doing work there and that I would be flying around the world for my business. I had never considered Portugal so I was very intrigued.

I realized that the angels had brought her to my life to be an angel here on earth, to be a resource for me, to support me, make me laugh and to kick my butt when I needed it. I realized I was supposed to keep her connected to who she is, to her spirit, and bring out the healer and lightworker in her. We were a good match.

Luckily for me, because of this new friendship, Nancy's husband, Dave, soon became a part of my life as well.

Chapter 32

My new job was challenging in many ways. I was determined to move the department to a more productive level. But no matter how hard I tried, I felt overwhelmed by the sheer amount of work. It was as if I were turning the Titanic around. There were so many things that weren't working that I felt like I had to be a hero to fix. While I loved the challenge of it, I didn't always like the responsibility. There was a lot for me to learn, and I began to doubt I had the ability or the desire to do it.

Every day I would pull an Angel Card from one of my many decks of oracle cards and every day I would do my darndest to fulfill the message of the day. Some days it was easy and some days it was hard. Every day I talked to my angels in the spirit world and my angel on Earth, Nancy.

I felt drawn to work with crystals more and more and to connect more with the angels. I had an amethyst, rose quartz and a clear crystal quartz at my desk and would set aside time every day to hold them and ask the angels for guidance. There was a lot of change happening around me. I was being drawn to new people, new friends and new situations. I could feel my energy shifting as I took on these new people and new situations.

During this time, I had also met a new friend Denise. Denise is a powerhouse and is someone who gets right to the point. She reminded me of the leader I am and worked with me to restore confidence in my leadership and power. She challenged me (and continues to do so) in many ways and never let me stay down. She brought structure to my life and helped me see things in a realistic way. Fortunately, she also encouraged me to see the humor in the situations that were upsetting me.

Denise and Nancy were now my closest friends and my "Angel Posse." They were two people who totally supported me and encouraged me to share my experiences as a lightworker despite my hesitation.

I also opened up to a few more people about the abilities I had kept hidden. It was like sharing it for the first time all over again. It was amazing to see how much I had kept hidden and kept secret out of a fear of exposing myself. Some people were intrigued and others were skeptical. The more I told people about it, the more it became real. The more it became real, the more I wanted to pursue it. I kept getting messages that this was what I needed to do full-time. I needed to leave my job, again. I needed to trust the guidance I was getting, but I felt that I wasn't ready. I needed more training. Yes, I had been doing readings and healings on people for years, and while I enjoyed it, I was not sure I could focus my whole life on that work.

Chapter 33

I frequently had thoughts about becoming a full-time lightworker and doing my healing work full-time. I tried to put those thoughts aside when I was at work, but doing that was really difficult. I figured that when the angels wanted me to begin to make a transition into a career as a lightworker, they would give me a sign. Boy, did they!

Everywhere I turned I started seeing references to Egypt. I turned on the History Channel and there would be a program on Egypt, its history and artifacts. The King Tut exhibit was in Philadelphia. I would open a book and on that open page would be something about the ancient Egyptians. Egypt, Isis and the mysteries of Egypt were coming up in an unusual number of random conversations. I was drawn to Lapis, a stone used by ancient Egyptians to denote power. It is also a stone that is used to enhance clairvoyance as well as to charge the Third Eye. This stone just resonated with me. It was weird. Egypt kept showing up everywhere. Isis had always been one of my guides so I asked her what was up.

I started having dreams about Egypt and the pyramids. The messages were getting loud and clear. I didn't know why or when but I knew I was going to Egypt - - someday.

But "someday" was not good enough for the angels. The angels kept talking to me about it, and the messages kept getting louder and louder. It was like I was being hit on the head with an etheric two by four. It was getting louder and louder and clearer and clearer that I needed to go. It also got louder and louder and clearer and clearer that I was not supposed to go by myself. Nancy was supposed to go with me. We were just starting to be friends so it seemed rather weird to me to ask her to go on a major trip with me.

However, I called her and I started the conversation with, "You are not going to like this." Nancy said, "What?" I said, "The angels want me to go to Egypt, and they want you to go with me." She paused and said, "I don't want to go to Egypt." My response to that was, "I got it. But they are not giving up until you go. There is something big happening in Egypt and they want both of us to go. They are not going to let up. In fact, they say it is critical that we go and we go now. Please say yes because it is getting painful." Twenty minutes later, we had our dates set – July 2007.

I did not know how I would come up with the money or time off from work to go on a 10-day trip to Egypt. I had just started this job and I didn't see how I could ask for time off. I kept hearing, "Trust. It will happen." Ok, angels, If I am supposed to go, do your thing! I asked them to guide me to show me the resources and to lead the way. I felt I needed to be there and, if that was the case, I knew they would come through for me. And they did!

Chapter 34

Every moment became a thought about Egypt. I was creating going to Egypt like crazy. It was another obsession, just as when I wanted to got to Greece. I found that I was doing research on Egypt every day. I love research like this, so I dug up lots of information about the pyramids, its art, culture and history. I had always liked Egyptian culture and art, but now it seemed magical. Like the Greek gods, I was fascinated by the Egyptian gods since childhood as well. By April I was totally excited about the trip but still needed a plan to come up with the money and time off from work. I trusted that Isis and Arch Angel Raphael, who is not only the angel of healing but also the angel of travel, would bring me the gold. I asked King Tut to share his treasures, and I just keep visualizing myself being there. I just knew it was going to happen. I could feel the energy building around me.

I was in one of my favorite stores with Nancy and we were looking at some stones and crystals to add to our ever growing collection. I spotted a beautiful, Lapis pyramid. I couldn't take my eyes off of it. I knew it was mine. I could feel Isis' super cool and powerful energy. It just spoke to me. I picked up the pyramid and held it for a few minutes. It started vibrating in my hand. I could not put it down. It was amazing.

I knew that I had to have this pyramid and that it would help me manifest my trip to Egypt. I looked at the price and nearly gasped. $120 for a rock???????? I put the pyramid down and then picked it up again. How could I spend $120 now if I needed to have money to go to Egypt?

I sat and contemplated for a few minutes. I could feel the power of the pyramid and I knew somehow it would help. But it seemed like a lot of money for a rock.

Nancy could see that I was really struggling with it. She said, "Get the pyramid. It will bring in more money and it will be a visual tool." She had said what I was thinking. So I took a big gulp, went to the cash register and paid.

I knew it was what I needed to do and was surprised that it worked so fast. When I got home, there was a check in the mail for $250 -- a rebate that I had forgotten about. I had already doubled the price of the lapis in a few hours. I could hardly wait to see what I would manifest in a few weeks. This was very exciting. I could see it was going to happen.

Chapter 35

Over the next few weeks, I kept telling everyone I met, whether I knew them or not, that I was going to Egypt. It was going to happen! I was excited and acting like it was a done deal. I would research every night when I got home from work. I would talk to Nancy every day about it. I think bets were on whether we would actually go, but I knew it was happening.

I started saying affirmations every day. "I am a money magnet and money comes to me naturally and freely." I began finding small amounts of money everywhere. I would look on the street and find money. I would find money in the dryers at the laundromat, and I would find money around the house and in my pants pockets.

I kept creating and creating like I have never created anything before. I would hold the pyramid every day and visualize walking the famous Giza Strip. I would ask Isis to work her magic. I carried that lapis pyramid everywhere with me. It was on my desk. It was on my nightstand. It was on my Third Eye when I meditated. I would look at it in the mornings when I woke up. I also think I even went to sleep with it in my hand sometimes.

I focused so hard on this trip. Well the rock paid off, literally. I received over a period of 3 weeks, $12,000. It seemed like it just showed up. I received money from my mother's estate, fees that people had owed me for past services, and even a few more forgotten-about rebates. It was magical how it showed up. It was enough to pay off my credit card, put some in the bank and pay for my trip to Egypt.

King Tut, here I come! Once the money was there, I worked out the dates with my boss. While I was going to be gone 10 days, I somehow managed to have only 5 of those days be vacation days. Everything was falling into place. I got the money, I got the time off, and my excitement rose.

It was not the first time the angels had come through when they had simply said, "Trust". I had learned to really listen when the angels say, "Trust". It always works out when I just surrender and trust. I don't have to make it so hard.

The trip was finally booked. We were rarin' and excited to go and counting the days. It seemed like we were never going to get there. I kept getting messages from Isis and knew she was going to be a critical part of my journey. She would appear in my dreams and give me insights about my trip. Her messages were always so clear and so encouraging and always such a reminder of the Egyptian past I was starting to remember. I knew I had some connection to Egypt that I was beginning to uncover. It was starting to look like I had been there before in another lifetime or perhaps many.

I knew that something BIG was going to happen for me on this trip. It was the same sensation before I went to Greece. I wasn't sure how it was going to play out, but I knew that the timing was right for the miraculous. The closer the trip came, the stronger the feelings became. I knew that I was creating what was next in my life as well as completing the past, both in this life and in past and parallel lives.

The night before we left, I was a little nervous, apprehensive, couldn't sleep and glad I had Nancy by my side with me on this trip.

Chapter 36

The day that we had been waiting for arrived. FINALLY! Nancy and I were both nervous and excited and had no idea what adventures and awakenings lay before us. We had both grown so much in the process of planning the trip, and we hadn't even left yet.

Our flight over was entertaining. We were served breakfast -- four times! We got a huge kick at that. As we were beginning our descent into Cairo, we could see the pyramids in the distance. It was real! We were here and it was exciting. I could not wait to see them up close.

After the long flight, we arrived in Cairo and were met by our escort, Mohammad. He took us to our hotel, the Mena House, and on the way explained that the Egyptian people didn't finish buildings completely so that they could avoid paying the taxes on them. They were finished on the inside but, on the outside, the top floor always was incomplete and made it look like an unfinished building. You would think that the government would catch on to this if EVERYONE was doing it. We passed by some beautiful areas where the wealthy lived that were just simply stunning. The Mena House was some distance from the airport so we had time to learn about areas of Cairo we would not have necessarily seen. We finally arrived at the Mena House Hotel which was guarded by guards out front and was so close to the pyramids that I felt like I could touch them. The Mena House was established in 1869 and has hosted many kings and emperors on their visits to Egypt. It is built on acres of Jasmine-scented gardens and is the most beautiful hotel I have ever seen. I thought about what it would be like to be married at this hotel. It is truly a palace. It overlooks the pyramids, it has marble floors and staircases and the longest hallway I had ever seen. The only drawback was walking that longest hallway to get to our room after a hot day of site-seeing. Regardless, the hotel was a magical experience for us. I felt like a princess.

We could not wait to get checked in, drop our stuff off, take a quick shower and head out to explore.

Despite our excitement, we were a bit nervous about leaving the grounds of the hotel. We had no idea how safe it was. It turned out to be incredibly safe. We wandered into a store selling Egyptian souvenirs. We looked at the papyrus paintings, smelled the oils, looked at and ordered cartouches with our names on them, and had a great conversation with the owner, all in the first 30 minutes after checking into our room.

After our first shopping adventure in Cairo, we roamed around the gardens of the hotel. We could see the pyramids and I felt as if I had come home. I was overwhelmed with emotion, happiness and gratitude. We just sat and looked at the pyramids for a moment in silence. It was something we had never experienced at that magnitude before. I was anxious to go to see them tomorrow. I could not imagine how the pyramids could get any more beautiful than they were in this single moment.

We wandered a bit more, had some dinner at an "authentic" Italian restaurant on the hotel premises. Inside we found the restaurant, named Saddles. It is decorated in a country and western style theme with a waiter playing the accordion and singing the tunes of Frank Sinatra. We were the only ones in there and were serenaded by "Frank" over and over. We were highly amused at the attempt of the Egyptian Frank Sinatra. We ate our "authentic" Italian dinner, which wasn't bad at all and made our way down the mile long hallway to our room. I think it took us an hour to get there. By the time we got there, we were spent. There was not one ounce of anything left in us. We went to sleep with visions of pharaohs dancing in our heads and thanking the angels for having us arrive safely. That night we had no trouble falling asleep.

Chapter 37

Nancy and I woke up at sunrise wide awake, without the alarm clock. We got dressed, ate a breakfast that consisted of eggs, fresh pineapple and watermelon, and then met our tour guide Hannan in the lobby. Arab Cairo is pretty conservative and much more conservative than we were used to. We were dressed in what we considered to be quite conservative attire for warm weather, capri pants and short sleeve tops.

Hannan, however, was dressed from head to toe, her whole body covered except for her hands and her beautiful Egyptian face. How could she stand it? It was so hot! Why we decided to go in July was a mystery to me. We were amazed that she could stand the heat in all that clothing. We were already dripping sweat in our capri pants, and it was still early in the morning.

Hannan told us the history of the various sites we were seeing along the way to Memphis, the ancient capitol of Lower Egypt. We were amazed at the everyday look of the city. People were riding camels and donkeys like it was the most natural thing in the world. There were people carrying palm fronds on wagons. It was definitely a different sight than we were used to seeing in New York City. I looked at Nancy and said "we're not in Kansas anymore!"

Hannan told us stories about some of the ancient Egyptian artifacts and how they were stolen from the Egyptian people. For example, how the head of Queen Nefertiti lies in the Museum of Berlin rather than Egypt, and the fact that the Egyptians are not very happy about that.

Hannan was very knowledgeable and very passionate about her country, and she delighted us with many amazing stories of the ancient world. By the time we arrived in Memphis, which is about an hour outside of Cairo, we felt like we had just done Egypt 101. Later, just for fun, Hannan quizzed us on what she had taught us in the morning. Boy was I glad it was for fun and not real! We really liked Hannan and felt blessed that she had been assigned to show us Cairo. The angels had done good.

When we got to Memphis, the first stop was a colossal Ramses statue that had been excavated a few years back. Ramses was the third pharaoh to rule Egypt and is considered by some to have been the most powerful ruler. He was renowned for being willing to make peace with his enemies. Obviously, Ramses was quite impressed with his own power and beauty; he commissioned many temples and monuments to commemorate his reign.

This colossal Ramses statue is enormously breathtaking. We stared at it from above and were amazed by the sheer dynamics of this one huge figure carved from a single piece of granite. There were many statues made in his honor, but this is the biggest and one of the most famous.

We were stunned at the enormity of it and enjoyed walking around comparing the size of our own body to that of the statue. One finger of the statue was the size of one of my legs.

The details were astonishing and the power was inescapable. We could feel the energy of this place as it ran up and down our spines, tingling us to the core.

Walking around the sacred grounds of Memphis, I felt surrounded by the energy of the ancient gods and goddesses. I knew their spirits were present. It brought a sense of peace to be there. The Egyptians had a connection to the spirit world that was lost, or rather suppressed, when the Romans conquered them. There were people who still practiced the ancient teachings despite being conquered. The history of the ancient Egyptians is very compelling and very spiritual. Seeing their structures and temples, I really got a sense of the spiritual beings the ancient Egyptians were. Each structure was impeccably built.

After we visited the plaza in Memphis and marveled at the giant statue of Ramses, we were off to the Saqqara Pyramid. This pyramid was the first step pyramid built in the world and was just stunning as the pictures we had seen. We were shown original columns that were built when the first Egyptians began building things. They amazingly were still intact. As we walked around the Saqquara pyramid complex, I got a sense of the sheer genius of the Egyptians. Brilliant does not even come close to describing them.

We strolled through the Royal courtyard and had visions of the ceremonies that took place there. The Saqqara Pyramid is a very healing and very powerful place. I spent some time in the courtyard by myself and could feel the energy rushing through my body. I found myself standing there with my eyes closed just allowing myself to receive the energy and the messages that were flowing to me. It became very clear to me that I had lived during this time period. I saw flashbacks to a time many, many years ago when I was living and working on this very same spot. I was a healer and was working with a guide to teach me. It was like I was being downloaded some symbols. Sacred Geometry perhaps? It was a time when Egypt was at the height of its power.

I could hear Nancy in the background calling my name. I opened my eyes and looked around. Apparently, I had been experiencing that vision for quite some time. Nancy had thought I was having a problem because of the heat and asked if I was ok. I told her I had just been receiving energy and I was fine. I knew we would speak more about it later when we weren't around Hannan. Nancy had learned by this point to trust me when I got guidance or messages.

As we left Saqqara one of my favorite incidents of the whole trip happened – one worth lots of retelling when I got home. An Egyptian man offered Nancy a camel if I would marry him. Come on, I thought I was worth way more than one camel! Nancy thought about it and decided we would go for something bigger. It was the first of many proposals that were made to me on that trip, each one getting bigger and more grandiose.

We were thirsty and made a stop at a carpet company nearby. You see, the Egyptians have enormous generosity and hospitality. They serve cold drinks to people who come into their store whether they purchase something or not. We did not purchase any of the beautiful carpets but we did enjoy the nice cold hibiscus tea.

After the tea, off to the Pyramids we went. Yippee! I had been waiting for this moment for a long time.

Chapter 38

As soon as I was close to the Pyramids of Giza and could see them, I squeaked with delight. I must have sounded like a kid seeing Mickey Mouse for the first time. I felt like I was home. I started crying tears of gratitude and joy. It was overwhelming to see the magnitude and the beauty of these three great structures. Pictures can't even begin to describe them. There are no words to explain how we felt as we stood at the base of the pyramid and looked straight up to the top. We gave Hannan our things and our cameras and we began to climb the rocks that led to the opening of the Great Pyramid, also known as the Pyramid of Cheops or the Pyramid of Khufu.

We climbed straight up the ramp inside the pyramid to get to the King's Chamber. It was a ramp that had wooden planks for steps and it was a trek to get up there. The ceiling was so low that we basically had to crawl up that ramp. It was so hot and steamy, that we had to pause frequently to drink water. We finally got to the King's Chamber and immediately sensed the vibrating energy of the space.

The room was perhaps 10x15 feet if that, and pretty dark. Only a small flash light that had been plugged into an extension cord that ran down to the ground outside provided the slight illumination by which we could explore the room. We walked to the sarcophagus and could feel the energy and the presence of something in the room with us, yet we were alone. We put our hands on the sarcophagus and just felt the powerful Egyptian energy emanating from it. We had expected to feel things while we were there because we were both sensitive to energies, but the power of what we were feeling was not expected.

We knew that each of the pyramids and temples lie along a chakra line, meaning that they resonate with each of the chakras. The Great Pyramid resonates with the crown chakra and each temple along the Nile resonates with a different chakra. Abu Simbel, the great temple south of Aswan, resonates with the root chakra.

We had planned to do a mini meditation at each temple to activate and clear the chakras. We sat with our back against the sarcophagus and our hands facing the top of the pyramid. I led us through a brief meditation, and then we just sat in silence reveling in the energy. We both opened our eyes and looked at each other not knowing what was happening. We felt the energy start to shift and knew something big was about to happen. We were a little nervous, but what happened was one of the most profound experiences of my life.

Suddenly, a giant column of white and purple light appeared right in front of us. It was a huge column, about two feet in diameter, and reminded me of a scene from Star Trek. As this bright, white and purple column descended, Nancy and I stared in disbelief. There was no one else in the chamber with us. A white feather floated down and this loud voice began to speak.

I knew it was Arch Angel Michael even before he spoke. He said, "My child, do not worry. You are protected here and I will guide you. This journey is the first of many, and your work with Egypt is just beginning. Trust. You are here for a reason. There will be many things that are accessed and gained on this trip and many things that are released. Do not be frightened. We are here. Peace be with you."

Then the white column disappeared, but the white feather remained. I picked it up and put it in my pocket as a reminder of the experience.

We sat there for a moment trying to get a grip around what had just happened. I looked at Nancy and she looked at me, and before I could ask if she had seen what I had just seen, she said, "Yep, I saw it too." We felt very blessed. If nothing else happened on the rest of my time in Egypt, this experience made the whole trip worth it.

I think we were both glad we had each other to verify the experience, because no one would have believed what had just happened.

We started crawling back down the ramp and talked about what we had just experienced. Believe it or not, crawling down the ramp was much harder than crawling up. It was so steep, almost straight down, and very hot. We could not wait to get down, get outside and stretch out our legs.

Hannan took some pictures of us coming out of the pyramid dripping wet with sweat. Believe it or not, it was cooler outside the pyramids. We then ventured to do the thing that I just HAD to do -- ride a camel at the pyramids. This was a must on my list in Egypt. My camel's name was Charlie Brown, a great American name for an Egyptian camel. I rode Charlie Brown for about 25 minutes, mostly in a state of sheer terror. His owner wanted me to run with him and gallop and I had a flashback of the raging beast, the donkey, running up the hill in Greece. NO WAY!

After my short but entertaining ride on Charlie Brown, we explored the other pyramids in the complex, the Pyramid of Khafre and the Pyramid of Menkaure. There are over 100 pyramids in Cairo but these three are the most famous.

Hannan told us of the thieves who had stolen the smooth limestone off the Giza pyramids to build their houses. The limestone was missing from all of the pyramids except the top of the Menkaure pyramid. Despite the Limestone missing, the pyramids were still breathtaking.

Chapter 39

Our next stop was the Great Sphinx, which is a lot farther away from the pyramids than it looks in pictures. The Great Sphinx is the guardian of the Giza pyramids and great he is. The mystery of how he was built and where he came from is even more of a mystery when taking into account its giant size.

We walked along the Sphinx complex and were stunned at the beauty that surrounded us. Underneath the Sphinx is rumored to be the Akashic records from the Atlantean times. When Atlantis was destroyed all the gods and goddess were dispersed to Greece and Egypt and became the rulers there. The records of the crystals and their energy were hidden under the Sphinx for protection.

Nancy and I stood next to the Sphinx absorbing the tons of energy coming at us, and we were overwhelmed at the experience we were having. We felt the ground move beneath us and swore it was an earthquake. We felt and heard the rumble. We looked around and no one seemed to notice so we thought maybe we were imagining it. We both felt it; we did not imagine it. We asked Hannan if she felt it, and she had said yes. We were not going crazy.

It was yet another experience we could not explain. I could feel the Egyptian gods and goddesses gathering around us. Their energy was swirling like the energy had at La Famiglia Sagrada in Barcelona. I saw the blue, green, gold and even purple energy around us. There energy is much different from that of the angels, yet also very powerful. I could feel them with us. I knew by Nancy's expression that she could too. We were fascinated by it all. Hannan told us more about which god and goddess ruled what and we learned about the studies and culture of the ancient civilization.

Hannan was very knowledgeable and proud about the ancient Egyptian culture. She also gave us a book to read that had the various Egyptian gods and goddesses in it. It was exciting to learn and expand our knowledge. I could feel Isis' energy coming in strong just as it had before we left New York. Clearly she was guiding me on this trip and clearly she had more work for me to do in Egypt.

There was a lot of information given to us that day, both from Hannan about the culture and the information we had received from the spirit world. It had been a very long day and we were tired. We went to have our dinner by the pool at the Mena House Hotel and watched the pyramids glow from the light and sound show that plays each night.

As we finished our dinner and went off to our room, we had a great conversation discussing the insights we were having about ourselves, why we were in Egypt and why we had to come on the trip together.

We saw that we were here to heal things from the past that were in the way of us creating a future. I discovered things that had been in the way of my being in a relationship. As much as I hated that conversation, I was grateful that I had Nancy to delve into this topic with me. I also saw how much I felt compelled to work with spirits and teach others. I got clearer and clearer that I wanted to open my school. Nancy and I discovered a lot about ourselves that night and each other. I knew that this was a friendship that was going to last a life time.

When we returned to our room I began writing postcards, but I was simply too tired and fell asleep in the middle of writing. I woke up around 3 am and put the postcards on the nightstand, turned out the light and had dreams of the magical time we had that day.

Chapter 40

The next morning began with an amazing breakfast consisting of the best watermelon I had ever tasted. The melons, from the fertile Nile Valley, were rich, sweet and full of flavor. They were delicious and just melted in my mouth.

After breakfast we met Hannan in the lobby. Hannan greeted us with a hug and we were off to the other side of Cairo to go to the Egyptian Museum with its displays of Egyptian artifacts and King Tut's treasures.

The air-conditioning was off in the museum, and it was the middle of July so you can imagine just how hot it was. The sweat was rolling off people, including Nancy and me.

We saw the mummies, the jewelry and the paintings. We saw the various statues that paid homage to the great rulers, kings and queens and learned more about the statues and their positions and what they represented in Upper and Lower Egypt. Hannan again quizzed us on the information that we had gathered over the last two days. It was fun to challenge our minds.

The best exhibit by far was King Tut's treasures. I am not sure if we enjoyed it so much because it was the only place in the museum that was air-conditioned, or because the artifacts were so unbelievably beautiful and intact. In preparation for my trip to Egypt, I went to the King Tut exhibit in Philadelphia. That exhibit was so impressive that I was certain there could not be much left in the Cairo museum. But I was wrong.

The museum in Cairo still had plenty to offer. We looked at the jewelry and were amazed that the Egyptians did not have back or neck aches since each piece looked like it weighed 20-50 pounds. We could feel Tut's energy as we examined the treasures he had left behind. He was a powerful and proud energy. I could almost feel his eyes gazing into the back of my head as we looked at his prized possessions. We explored the Tut exhibit for at least an hour and then completed our visit by touring the rest of the museum.

After the museum, we went to the Citadel Mosque. From the mosque we could view the city of Cairo and the pyramids which served as a spectacular backdrop to the cityscape. It was such a contrast to have a huge modern city with several ancient pyramids floating in the background. It was definitely not something you would see in New York!

The mosque was beautiful with all of its gold trim and marble tiles. The gates were beautiful, intricately molded iron. Nancy and I took a few moments of fun and dressed up as belly dancers in front of the Mosque. The Citadel had a photo setup where visitors could rent costumes for photos. We struck all kinds of poses and had a great laugh at each other in our Egyptian getup. We had fun dressing and posing in our glittery belly dancing outfits.

On the way out, we walked through a neighboring market and enjoyed picking up neat little Egyptian souvenirs. We bought carved wood items including a camel for my father's carved wood collection. We bought silver charms for a charm bracelet. We bought beautiful flowing scarves and much, much more. While we were shopping, we befriended a cat who decided it would be a really great idea to come home with me. He climbed up my leg and into my bag and meowed like crazy. As much as I wanted to take him home, I left him at the market. Besides all the logistical matters of getting him out of the country, quarantine and smuggling him on the airplane, I seem to be bound by my cat Zoe's one cat rule.

After the market at the Citadel, we went to look at some of the jewelry in the Egyptian stores. I wanted a signature piece of jewelry to remind me of my trip and to add to my collection of 'travel' jewelry, pieces I collect from my travels. I was looking for something like an Isis or Maat pendant that would be unique to Egypt but also classy and elegant. I could feel Isis' power and wanted something to remind me of her. I tried on many pendants of both Isis and Maat and none of them seemed quite right. It just didn't match what I wanted or was looking for.

Nancy saw a pendant of the Eye of Horus set in white gold with an emerald for the green eye. She had the jeweler make it in yellow gold for me with a ruby for the eye. When I saw it, I knew it was exactly the piece I was looking for. When the jeweler finished making it, I put it on and wore my Eye of Horus with pride, knowing I was totally protected. It was the perfect piece of jewelry for me to take home.

We had one more scheduled stop for the day and that was Khan El Khaili market. This market is famed for its tight spaces, many haggling merchants and inexpensive but beautiful merchandise. We went from store to store, bargaining and looking for things we wanted to bring back home. We learned a big lesson. As is the case in many countries, tourists are charged more than the natives. Hannan could get us things at a much lower cost with much less effort. We learned to have her use her bargaining skills for us.

That night, we were being treated to a light show at the pyramids. It was the history of the Pharaohs, the pyramids and the Sphinx told in great detail, with light, sound and lasers. It was quite a story and a beautiful experience.

It had been quite a day. We had shopped 'til we dropped at the market, learned the history of all the dynasties at the museum and learned about the Islamic culture at the Citadel.

The next day was to begin very early with a sunrise air flight to Luxor. So we packed our things that night, set the alarm for 3 am, and went to bed. It seemed like it was only minutes after I fell asleep that the high pitched beep of the alarm was awakening us.

Chapter 41

We jumped out of bed, showered and went downstairs to meet Mohammad. He had gotten our breakfast boxed up for us, and we got into our car to go to airport. People were still out and partying in Cairo. We checked in at the airport for our crack of dawn flight to Luxor and had plenty of time before our flight took off. We fought to stay awake until we boarded our plane. We took off as a beautiful sun rose over the Sahara and painted the desert many colors.

We arrived in Luxor around 9 am and were met by our guide for the day, Wael. He took us directly to our cabin on our Nile riverboat, the Sun Princess, and helped us get our things set up there. He then offered to take us around Luxor via horse and carriage. We thought that would be an interesting way to spend the day.

We got to see all the sights of Luxor beyond the wealthy area that rested on the banks of the Nile. We rode out to the country with me sitting in front of the carriage with the driver. We stopped by a local farmer's house for some hibiscus tea to cool us down. Nancy rode a camel that happened to belong to the farmer. He wasn't as cute as Charlie Brown but was quite entertaining.

When we got back in the carriage Nancy and Wael were sitting together in the back of the carriage laughing and having a good time. Nancy was telling Wael about the man who wanted to give her a camel in exchange for marrying me. Nancy jokingly told Wael that she had seriously considered the offer. I don't think Wael thought she was joking because he suddenly started making passes at me and asking me to spend the afternoon with him. It became uncomfortable for me, and I think that Nancy sensed it. She abruptly changed the subject and kept diverting the conversation away from me. We stopped to have an Egyptian treat, sugar cane juice, which later proved to be a "death juice" for Nancy and me.

Wael dropped us back at the boat and I made an excuse for something and went inside. I wanted to get away from Wael as fast as I could since I felt creepy around him. When I was out of earshot, he asked Nancy what she thought about him taking me out to dinner and then a night on the town. She told him politely that she did not think it would be a good idea, thanked him for the tour and walked away. That was the end of Wael.

Chapter 42

We went to our cabin and took a long and deep nap after our day of sightseeing. We had only planned to sleep for about an hour or so but were startled awake when the phone rang at 10 minutes 'til 3. It was the captain letting us know our tour to Luxor and Karnak temples was beginning in ten minutes. We scrambled out of bed, brushed our teeth and did as much else as we could in that short amount of time.

We scurried to our bus and were excited to be on the way to the Luxor Temple. The temple is massive and beautiful. Original paintings still decorate the ceilings and original statues are in place throughout the temple. We were particularly amazed at the detailed decorations on the columns of the temple. As I said before, the temples on the Nile lie on an energy grid that works and tunes the chakras. This temple is the temple that resonates with the Third Eye chakra.

Nancy and I were looking for the perfect place to do a meditation. As we searched for a spot, we talked about the energies we were experiencing. I could feel it pulsating against my body and invigorating my mind. Nancy's experience was one of being soothed and relaxed.

We both were drawn to a particular column in the middle of the temple. It was right in the sunlight and we sat there, Nancy and I on opposite sides, allowing our Third Eye to be filtered, activated and cleaned from the powerful Egyptian sun and the Sun God Ra. The energy was very strong and intense as it poured into my body. We each did our own meditation silently and took a few moments to allow the Third Eye to open further so we could receive more information. I could see swirls of indigo blue, purple and white light around me. It was a very powerful time for me, and Nancy said it was equally powerful for her. I saw again that I had more work to do in Egypt and that I would be guided and would know when the time was right. I also saw more work in writing and healing in other countries that was coming my way. I saw me teaching in Greece, in India and perhaps Mexico. I knew to trust the information we received from Isis and Ra during this meditation. It was a very calming and peaceful meditation. Afterwards we both instinctively put our hands on the column when we were done; we immediately both got flashes from past lives in Egypt.

We had similar visions. We saw that Nancy had been a prominent priest or religious figure at this temple, and I was an artist that carved the hieroglyphics. It seemed as if we had worked together and had spent many times and many hours in this temple in our past. We spent a few moments reflecting on our visions and after a while, we made our way back to the bus.

Our next destination was the Temple of Karnak, but Nancy was starting to feeling sick. I wasn't sure if it was the heat or her past life vision that was having her not feel well. I got her some water and a wet paper towel and had her lay down on the bus. I sent her Reiki, did a mini-healing on her and pulled out any energy blocks I could see.

My Third Eye has always been fairly open, and after our meditation in the temple, it seemed as if things were even glowing brighter now. I sent her light and energy but she was getting paler and paler as the moments passed. I was afraid she was going to pass out. I could see blocks of energy that were pent up in and around her. We talked about what I was seeing and how it was holding her back in all areas of life. I asked her if I could remove them and she said yes. She instantly started to feel a little better and I told her to keep drinking the ice cold water to keep her cool and nourished. It was hot, and the cold water seemed to make a huge difference.

Nancy felt much better after a few minutes, so we continued on to the Temple of Karnak. The Temple of Karnak is just as beautiful as the Temple of Luxor. We walked around the temple and came across a reflection pool that reflects a stunning mirror image of the temple and palm trees swaying in the background. It is truly breathtaking and very peaceful to gaze into it. There is also a giant scarab in front of the pool, which is an Egyptian symbol for luck. Walking around it numerous times is supposed to bring luck and wealth. Although we are not superstitious, we began walking around it; thinking a little bit of extra luck couldn't hurt anyone.

We found a lovely place to sit in the shade by a sphinx and decided to do our meditation there. We did work on the ear chakra to open ourselves up to any messages we needed to receive. Many messages began to come to me.

I received messages from many of the Egyptian gods and goddesses, the Greek gods and goddesses, the Atlantean deities, the angels and the ascended masters. I felt like I had a huge army telling me what to do. There was so much going on, I had to ask them to slow down. They were so excited. I could feel Isis and Horus welcoming me home. I knew that Arch Angel Michael was speaking to me and telling me that this was the beginning of a new path. I heard Arch Angel Ariel say, "Courage. It is time to spread your wings and fly." It seemed like they were talking to me for hours, but when I looked at my watch, I saw that it had only been about ten minutes. There was so much information coming at me that, although it was exciting, it was also overwhelming. I knew they were all excited and talking to me about my work as a lightworker. Except this time, when I was being told what do, I wasn't annoyed. They were definitely giving me lots of guidance to assimilate.

Nancy, however, started feeling ill again and this time it was worse than it had been before. I suddenly had a concern about getting her back to the bus. I got her to a bathroom, where I paid the attendants 20 Egyptian pounds for toilet paper, and then ran to get her a bottle of fresh water. You don't pay for the bathroom in Egypt; you pay for the toilet paper. From then on we always made sure we had our own toilet paper wherever we went.

We got her back to the bus and boat safely. When we got back to our boat, we immediately went to our cabin to cool down and rest before dinner. The cabin was air-conditioned and it was literally a breath of fresh air after being in the desert. When Nancy and I went down to the dinner table, we were not hungry at all but knew we needed to eat something. I didn't feel so well myself at this point. I was nauseated and had a bad stomach ache. Fortunately one of the items on the menu was chicken soup. Both of us had the chicken soup and the fruit plate to eat, hoping it would soothe our aching bellies.

We debated on whether we should go straight to bed or stay up to watch the belly dance performance. We decided that since we didn't have the opportunity to see a live belly dancer that often, we should stay up a little while to see her perform.

We watched her dance and were pretty disappointed. I was expecting much more glitz, much more glamour, much more sensual dancing than the basic moves she attempted, the kind of belly dancing you see in the movies. After all this was Egypt. We expected to see some exotic dancer with long flowing black hair and mysterious eyes dancing, not the overweight woman in front of us.

She decided to enliven her act by pulling people up from the audience to dance with her. She tried to pull me up, but I felt so ill with my rotten stomach ache that I resisted. Instead, she pulled up a 12-year old girl from Dubai, Hadil, who ended up dancing circles around her. I think the performer was so upstaged by Hadil that she ended her show early. I much more enjoyed watching Hadil dance throughout the rest of the night.

By the time we returned to our cabin we were both sick as a dog. We tried to figure out what had made us so sick. We had been very careful to drink nothing but bottled water, so we didn't think it could have been that. Then it dawned on us -- The Sugar Cane Death Juice we had drunk earlier that afternoon. It dawned on us that it was a root, pulled from the ground and then juiced. Arghh, mystery solved. Note to self: Do not drink Sugar Cane Death Juice offered from strange Egyptian men named Wael again.

Chapter 43

We woke up the next morning at 4 am to start our next adventure in Egypt. We had booked a sunrise hot air balloon ride over the West Bank. We both felt somewhat better after the Death Juice was leaving our system but still had a question if there was any remaining. We took some medicine as we had a thought that being up in a hot air balloon was not the best place to have an upset stomach hit.

We got to the boat that was going to take us across to the west bank of the Nile. It was still dark outside and everyone was not quite awake yet. As we boarded the boat, the crew shouted, "Wakie, Wakie," and handed us a hard roll and tea. They were awfully chipper for that time of the morning as they sang traditional Egyptian songs to get us going.

The boat ride to the west bank took about 15 minutes. We got out of the boat and watched with awe and excitement as the balloons were being blown up. My excitement and nervousness was building. There must have been 20 or so hot air balloons being blown up and about 200 people waiting.

We finally were given the go ahead to board our balloon and waited in anticipation until we floated into the sky. It was breathtaking to see the Nile and the Valley of the Kings and Queens from the air at sunrise. The bright morning sunlight shining on the Nile was magnificently reflected back up to us in our balloon.

The sun was rising fast, and so was the temperature. I was standing under the flame of the balloon and started to feel dizzy and queasy. I was getting so hot and so uncomfortable and felt like I was going to pass out any moment. I had never felt anything like this. Nancy kept saying, "Look up, Look up" I finally grabbed a cold water bottle from the cooler on board the balloon and sat on the floor. I called on the angels and the Egyptian gods and anyone else who could keep me from passing out. I drank the ice cold water and sat on the bottom of the balloon for about 10 minutes to recover and then I was fine. I enjoyed the trip immensely except for that 10-minute spell of dizziness and nausea.

When the balloon landed, the natives pulled me out and danced with me. It was only around 6 am and they were a jolly bunch. It was quite humorous to be dancing with this mix of native Egyptians and tourists and proved to be great fun. We danced until the car pulled up to take Nancy and me on our next adventure -- the Valley of Kings, Queens and Hatshepsut's Temple.

Our first stop was the Valley of the Kings. We were allowed to go to three of the tombs of the Kings, not King Tut's tomb unfortunately because they were filming a documentary. The walls were painted and designed beautifully for the royals that had once been buried there. Again, as in the previous day's temples, I was amazed at the detailed drawings and hieroglyphics. There was so much detail and so many inscriptions in hieroglyphic form and it was all perfectly chiseled and painted.

Other than the still existing wall paintings, there were very few artifacts remaining in the tombs. I assumed everything that had once been in the tombs had been stolen long ago by thieves or removed to museums. The only remaining relic was an empty sarcophagus.

I could not fathom being one of the slaves who had built these tombs. They started constructing the tomb as soon as the king or queen was in power and often finished them after their demise. Because the embalming and the mummification process was so rigorous it gave them a little time. The labor involved in going up and down the many stairs and ramps in all that heat must have been extremely intense.

We had poured the water from one of our water bottles on our heads to cool us off. So much for our hair! We sat in silence for a few minute resting and trying to cool off as much as we could. I put a wet washcloth on my neck to cool down. I stared in awe at all the tombs that were before me. I could not believe how many tombs had been built for the kings. There were over 100!

As we walked out, I got proposed to again, this time for 2 million camels. The stakes were getting much higher!

We drove down the road to the Valley of the Queens. These women of power were just as interested in leaving great tombs to honor them as the men had been. This valley was more open than the Valley of the Kings with fewer tombs built into the hills. There was also much more of a breeze coming from the Nile to cool us down.

We went first into the tomb of Nefertari and were stunned again at the amount of work that had to be done to complete this tomb.

I could feel the energy of Queen Nefartari, and hers was a powerful force. I saw all this purple energy circling around us as we were in her tomb. When we walked by and visited other tombs in both the Valley of the Kings and Queens, the energy was just as palpable, yet it was very distinct. It is a very sacred ground to walk on and the amount of energy that we felt was overwhelming and healing at the same time.

We went next to Hatshepsut's Temple. The native Egyptians called it "Hot Chicken Soups" Temple. The natives make a joke and call it this because they think Hatshepsut is hard for tourists to pronounce. This enormous structure is the temple of the throat chakra and is the only temple that is two stories. It was so hot I felt that I might melt like the witch in *The Wizard of Oz*.

I sat in the temple for a few minutes to do my meditation and to cool off. I had a washcloth saturated with water on my neck. I sat in silence and within a few minutes I felt this massive swirl around my throat area. I usually don't have a problem communicating, so I didn't know why I was having sensations of blocked communication. Then I heard loudly and clearly "It is time for you to speak your truth. You have been denying who you are, and it is time to go forward. We will guide you and the messages will be clear. It is up to you to listen and act on them." My heart felt so vulnerable and so open. I took many deep breaths and let out many sighs of release. As I breathed, I imagined any resentment, regret and anger I had leaving me. I sat there for a moment not quite sure what had happened. I looked around and everything seemed normal. I pondered what it meant to "speak my truth," and realized that I had some real thinking to do if I wanted to understand the messages I had just gotten.

One of the messages I was getting right then was very clear. I wanted ice cream.-- Now!

I went to find Nancy and our guide for the day Ahmed, and all I could speak was "ice cream." Nancy laughed and said, "It is only about 7:30 am." I said, "I don't care. Give me ice cream now or someone will die. I know of a few good tombs close by to dispose of the body" They laughed as we made our way up to the entrance of the temple. There was a café there and another opportunity for tourists to buy Egyptian merchandise and deal with the store owners who always want you to "please, visit my shop." Nancy and Ahmed had soda and I had ice cream. Twice. What can I say? It was really hot, and I really wanted ice cream.

Our guide, Ahmed was funny and easy to get along with, not to mention very handsome. He gave us so much information about the Kings, Queens's tombs and "Hot Chicken Soup's" temple that we hit brain overload.   He was gracious, knowledgeable and patient, and he must have wondered about this crazy American woman eating ice cream this early in the morning. But, he was nice.

He took us back to the small boat so we could cross the Nile to the port where our boat was docked. It was so hot and humid and it was almost 120° degrees (Fahrenheit) at 8:30 am! Being from New York, we were not used to this kind of extreme temperature. Nancy had lived in Arizona and I had lived in the Tennessee and Alabama but with the heat index, it was like 150°, which neither of us had experienced.

It was so nice to get back to our air-conditioned cabin on the boat. We took off our sopping wet smelly, clothes and put on dry clothes and went to the deck and had some cold juice. We'd already had an amazing day and it was still early morning!

Our boat sailed at 9:30 am, and we were lucky. The boat held 235 people but there were only about 45 people on board, so it was almost like having it to ourselves. Since it was a small group, we got to know other people. We were known by all as the "American women" because we were the only Americans on the boat. There was a family from Dubai, a couple from Brazil, a newlywed couple from London and the bride's father from India, a woman and her niece from Alexandria, Egypt and a huge contingency from Mexico.

We sat in the air-conditioned lounge playing cards, eating snacks, and watched the Nile go by. Our new friends were teaching us card games from their cultures, and it was funny to see them try to explain to Nancy and I how to play. I swear Nancy cheated although she denies it. It was fun getting to know the other passengers and sharing stories about ourselves and our countries.

We enjoyed the scenery of the Nile. On the west, there was pure desert, on the east, lush jungle.

At lunch, I shared with Nancy my message from Hatshepsut's temple and she was not surprised. We were both clear that this trip was bringing clarity to our lives and our purpose. After lunch, which was served at noon, we went to our cabin to take a 'brief' nap. A few minutes before dinner, the phone rang. It was the captain saying he was waiting on us to start dinner and were we coming? Nancy told them to start without us but they wouldn't hear of it. So we dressed quickly and went downstairs to the dining table. We had our own table so it was surprising to us that they were waiting. We could not believe we had slept from about 1 o'clock until dinner time. We had been hot and tired and dealing with the lingering aftermath of the infamous Death Juice.

Chapter 44

When we woke up the next morning, we were in Edfu. Since the only way to get to the temple is by walking a long way or by horse and buggy, we opted for the buggy. It was a tiny carriage, much smaller than the one we spent the day in during our stay at Luxor. Given the roads were cobble stone and gravel, it was a bumpy ride. Fortunately we only had to bump along for about 15 minutes.

This temple was dedicated to the God Horus. Horus is the God of Protection and is often represented by a falcon head or a single "eye." Remember, I bought a necklace in one of the markets that represents the "Eye of Horus." It is a very powerful symbol in the Egyptian culture. Horus was the son of Isis and Osiris and during a battle with the God of Destruction, Seth, Horus lost an eye. Isis later healed his eye, and therefore, the "Eye of Horus" became a symbol of power, healing, and protection.

This was my favorite temple so far. It was the most preserved and contained the most powerful energy I had felt. Nancy and I walked through the temple and put our hands on various columns receiving the messages and feeling the healing energy. Like the other temples we had visited, it was a very healing temple. It was also a peaceful, powerful and a very loving energy. We just felt safe and protected.

Between the energy of Horus that had been with me since I bought my necklace in Cairo and the energy of Arch Angel Michael with us, I knew we were in good hands. We walked around the temple looking for the perfect place to sit and do our meditation. This temple was aligned with the heart chakra and I could already feel the heart chakra trying to balance and sort itself out before we even sat down. Nancy wanted to explore and go someplace and do her own mediation, so we made our plans to meet back up at a particular column.

I sat at my column and felt something come over my body. As I sat there, I began weeping. I just sobbed for no reason. It was clear I was releasing something, but I had no idea what, and I didn't question it. I just sat there until the tears stopped. It felt like it was something beyond my control.

I just sat in the swirl of energy and didn't say anything. I let them do their thing. I had a piece of rose quartz in my pocket and held it tightly. The experience lasted about five minutes. Whatever it was, it was powerful and very healing. I felt my heart open and release. It was as if a ton of bricks had been removed and I was light, very light and very light-headed.

I finished the meditation and took out my water bottle for a drink and gulped down a few sips of water. I was clear that I was going to need to replenish my thirst after that one.

When I met back up with Nancy, I felt that I had released lifetimes of pent up energy. She looked different, I looked different, and the temple looked different. Something had happened. My heart was filled with love and I felt happiness around me. It was a peace I had not experienced in a long time.

I felt very fulfilled and content as we walked back to the carriage. This temple had been so impactful to me. I felt Horus' protective energy surrounding me, and I felt Isis' magical energy in every step I took. Nancy had a similar experience and both of us were in a very relaxed, peaceful state.

When we got back to the boat, we were bombarded by local store owners wanting to sell us goods and bottles of water for $100 USD. Yeah, right. I wasn't that thirsty.

We sat up on the rooftop deck of the boat watching the peaceful calm waters of the Nile go by. On the right side of the boat we saw hippos and cows bathing as we drifted by. We were on our way to Komombo, the Temple of the Crocodile. We had a few hours before our arrival so Nancy and I and our new friends sat by the pool enjoying the scenery of the Nile.

When we got to Komombo, we had given up on the conservative look completely and put on our tank tops and shorts. It was too hot to be pretending to look conservative.

At the Temple of Komombo, we were amazed by the mummified crocodile they had on display. It was an actual crocodile that had been mummified many years ago. The flowers that surrounded this temple created a lushness that none of the other temples we had visited had. We saw the first calendar ever made, as well as the fertility graph used to predict the sex of unborn children. There was also the Nilometer which the ancient Egyptians used to measure how much the Nile River was going to flood during the rainy season. They were brilliant.

I sat in a corner and did my meditation for the solar plexus chakra. I put my hands on my abdomen. I was overwhelmed by emotion and an amazing warmth emanated from my solar plexus. I saw all this yellow bright light, and it felt as if a hand were inside my system and spinning and clearing the chakras manually. I felt as if I was releasing all the old belief systems that had held me back. A whoosh of happiness and joy washed over me. I also felt extremely creative in that moment, like I could create anything. I started getting new ideas for what my life was going to look like. I started having the urge to listen to music and to paint, and I started to laugh, a real belly laugh that released the remains of lifetimes of energy.

I found Nancy and our new friends and we headed back to the boat. That night we were having a Galabaya party. A Galabaya is a dressy robe worn by Egyptians. So the idea of the party was to dress as glamorously as possible. Nancy and

I had actually bought Galabayas in Cairo in anticipation of the party. However, one of the men from Mexico had bought the exact one that Nancy had bought and was wearing daily. Nancy refused to show up at the party with the same 'dress' on as one of the men so we ended up renting ours from the boat. They were much prettier and much better looking than ours, so we were happy.

We adorned ourselves with beads and scarves and applied makeup that made us look like Cleopatra. We ate dinner on the roof deck and danced to Egyptian music until the wee hours of the morning. By now the Death Juice had left our systems completely and we were ready to be taught belly dancing by our 12-year-old friend, Hadil. She was quite good. There is something about the Egyptian music and the movement of the belly that is very sensual. I think it is more sensual to do it than to watch it. We laughed and laughed as we danced the night away.

After the party, Nancy and I got out of our Egyptian clothing and sat up on the roof deck under the stars. They were so beautiful and so bright. It was just the two of us and yet we were surrounded by the spirit that is Egypt. It was truly magical, every moment of it. I was so happy to be there and experience what I was experiencing and so happy to have Nancy with me. We connected in a way I have never connected with another human being. We could sense each other's energy and even began communicating somewhat telepathically.

We watched in awe as the boat's crew came to take the chairs, umbrellas and everything on the deck down. We asked why they were doing this, and soon found out that we were crossing under a bridge that was so low nothing could be above deck level. We thought this would be interesting to see so we laid down flat on the chairs and watched in amazement as we went under a bridge with just inches between the bridge and our noses.

We said goodnight to Isis, Maat, Horus and the rest and went to our cabins for a good night's sleep. It had been a long, exciting day and the next day was going to be just as big.

Chapter 45

We woke up the next morning in Aswan, in Lower Egypt. It was a very cultured area and the largest city we had seen since Cairo. It was a beautiful morning with a slight breeze, a perfect day to visit the Aswan Dam. This dam was built to help regulate the flow of the Nile to keep it from flooding and destroying the crops that grow in the fertile Nile Valley.

Nancy and I and our new friends, sat there for a few moments looking at the beauty that was around us. Below the dam was the scenery we had seen for all the days of our cruise along the Nile: the desert to the west and the jungle to the east. Above the dam was a huge lake extending south as far as we could see. The remains of a few small temples dotted the horizon.

We had some fun at the dam and then the next site we explored was on an island accessible only by boat, the Temple of Philae. This temple resonates with the sacral chakra and is dedicated to the goddess Isis, who had become my special guide on this trip. The temple was inundated by rising waters after the Aswan Dam was built in the 1960's. But before the temple could be totally lost, the island was surrounded by a dam and the water was pumped out. The temple was labeled, disassembled and then reassembled in exact order on the higher island of Agilka. The project to save this most beautiful temple from destruction took over ten years.

Initially the island of Agilka seemed to contain only ruins which looked like nothing more than piles of dirt. However, as we turned a corner, we saw the magnificent beauty of the temple and were blown away by the fierce energy that encompassed it. I walked around Philae and was clear; this by far was now my favorite temple. It was surrounded by the lushness of palm trees, beautiful red and purple flowers and the water of the Nile. There was a wonderful breeze which only made the experience better.

Nancy and I found a stairway leading down to the river and cooled our feet in the Nile's soothing waters. We sat there for a few minutes and let the river take away whatever it would. I felt that as it washed over our feet, it carried away all the excess energy that was there. There was such a strong vibration in the water. We felt as if our troubles (what was left of them) were pulled away. We sat there and just enjoyed the scenery and power around us.

I was nervous to do the meditation on the sacral chakra as I could already feel things happening and I had not even sat down to meditate yet. My sacral chakra felt blocked and definitely felt as if I were holding onto some things that I was not ready to confront.

I asked the angels to be with me because I knew that this meditation could be quite a release. I found a place that was dark and out of the way. Nancy went to her own spot, and I began my meditation. I closed my eyes and felt these giant wings around me as Isis told me to "take a deep breath." I did, and I just felt like crying again so I did. I had balanced my chakras many times before so I didn't have any clue as to why this trip was having them balance at a deeper and more emotional level. It took about seven minutes for Isis to do her thing. I just let her take over as I saw the bright orange light of the sacral chakra surround me. I knew I was safe as I watched beliefs, blocks and energy leave my body to be transmuted to the Universe.

I definitely opened something up, because as we left the temple, I received another marriage offer, this time for 7 million camels. I was definitely becoming more desirable the longer we stayed in Egypt! This was by far the best offer we had received, and Nancy was definitely considering taking this offer. Her only concern was the amount of camel poop that came with 7 million camels and how she was to get the camels back to Connecticut.

We still had a few minutes before we had to be back to our boat, so I began strolling around the market. I wanted ice cream and for three dollars bought myself something that resembled a Nestle Drumstick. Hadil, our new friend from Dubai, came up right after me with the exactly same ice cream for which she had paid fifty cents! I began to think hmmmmmm, "What if I give Hadil my money and she uses her innocent 12-year-old's charm to get better deals. I told Nancy about my plot, and she thought it was great. Then we told Hadil's parents Artem and Imani that we wanted to take Hadil shopping with us. We had become good friends with Artem, Imani, Arden (Hadil's adorable and charming brother) and Hadil. They were such a sweet family. Artem was the ambassador of tourism for Dubai. They laughed at our idea, but Hadil was very excited. Our plan was that when either of us saw something we liked, we would call out to the other, "Hey! Look at this!" We would meet, have a "conversation," scratch our heads and then walk away. A few moments later, Hadil would go look at it, pick it up and start bargaining with the merchant and purchase the item. This plan worked great until Hadil ran out of money. When we met to give her more money, the store owner saw the exchange, and our secret was exposed.

We went back to the bus with our Egyptian loot and traveled to the Aswan quarry to see the unfinished obelisk. The pink granite obelisk was started thousands of years ago but never finished because of a crack that occurred as they tried to carve it from the cliff. So it is still embedded in the side of the quarry only three quarters finished. It was neat to see, but whoever decided we should visit a rock quarry in the desert in the middle of the day should have been shot.

That afternoon, the family from Dubai invited Nancy and I to go with them to the Aswan market to do some shopping. This time we made sure Hadil had enough money to have our plan work. We also had our new Egyptian friend Joy with us. Joy was cool. She was a little younger than Nancy and I and was very pretty. She looked like an ancient Egyptian goddess with her long black hair and super-tanned skin. With so many people in our group who spoke Arabic, we figured we were assured of getting the best shopping deals possible.

Artem even developed our plot a bit further, telling shop owners, in Arabic mind you, that I was his new sister-in-law and I was to have anything I wanted at Egyptian prices. He said I had just married his brother and we were here on vacation. His brother, my apparent new husband, was resting and did not join us. Now, I did not know Artem was telling this story until later. I was just surprised at my new bargaining power. It wasn't until we had gone to four or five stores that I knew what Artem was saying. After that I could barely control my laughter as he cajoled the vendors into giving us the best deals possible for the new wife of his brother.

That afternoon we did something that was one of the highlights of the trip. We took a ride on a felucca sailboat at sunset. Our party was made up of the Dubai family, the Brazilian couple, the family from India, Joy, Joy's Aunt Laila, Nancy and me. We also had an Egyptian musician who played his tambourine and flute as we danced to his Egyptian rhythms. This was the perfect way to end the day. We sailed around Elephantine Island, where the botanical gardens are. We danced, we sang, we laughed. We saw the moon rise in the most spectacular setting I have ever seen. It was perfect. Every moment of it was just incredible.

The felucca brought us back after about two hours of sailing. We had limited time to get ready for dinner. This, our last night aboard, consisted of dinner, dancing and a Nubian show presented by local Nubians. Nancy and I were having such a great time and didn't want it to end.

The Nubian show was amazing with the dancing and drumming. We were highly impressed and quite entertained. The Nubian chief pulled Nancy out and did a sacrificial ritual dance with her. I have never laughed so hard. Luckily it was part of the show and he didn't really offer her up to any gods.

We danced until we couldn't dance anymore. It had been such an incredible adventure and one I would never forget. But the evening did come to an end. Sadly, we said goodbye to the new friends we had grown to love like family and went upstairs to pack. The next morning we would fly to Abu Simbel to see the temple and then return to Cairo.

That night Nancy and I talked about our trip, what we had experienced and what we had accomplished. We were clear about the messages we had received that my work in Egypt was just beginning. Nancy had gotten a message that day at Philae and was just now telling me. I have learned to trust

Nancy's messages just as much as she has learned to trust mine. She said that she saw that her purpose was to keep me grounded so that my work be powerful and not weird. She also got that I was supposed to take similar journeys there and have people awaken at a vast level. She got this look on her face and suddenly started channeling and said, "The world needs you now and I am here to support you. You can't give up. This journey is just the beginning and we are in this together." I knew just what she was talking about. I also saw her switch back to Nancy from the deity she was channeling. She knew she had just said something profound but had limited recall of what she'd said. It was a profound moment in time for both of us.

I was amazed to look back through my journal and see how much we had both grown from the amazing experiences we'd had. I knew neither of us were the same human being that had left New York, and that from that moment on, our life would not be the same.

We packed our things, turned out the light and went to bed. The next morning came very early and we were not ready for it.

Chapter 46

We woke up early in the morning and finished packing, had breakfast and said goodbye to our newfound friends as this would probably be the last time we would see them.

We went to the airport and boarded a plane to Abu Simbel. The temple is south of Aswan and I slept for the entire one-hour flight. We arrived in Abu Simbel and met our guide Athem who, during the tour, told us the history of the temple. We took many pictures of the colossal monument. This was the biggest temple of all. It, like other temples and monuments, had been reassembled on higher ground to save it from the rising waters of the lake formed by the Aswan Dam. Originally, it had been carved into a mountain. It was recreated exactly as it had been, including the positioning of one of the heads that had fallen during an earthquake.

We took some pictures that we hoped would show the huge scale of the statues. I was wearing a black shirt so you could easily see me in the photo. I am this tiny black dot in the bottom of the photo. It was huge and just as beautiful and amazing as it was big. This was the temple we were told not to miss, and after seeing it, we could understand why. It held the access to the root or base chakra which is where survival lives.

Our guide left us to explore the site on our own and arranged to meet us later for our trip back to the Cairo airport. Abu Simbel consists of two stone structures, one for Queen Nefertari and the other for King Ramses. We first went into Queen Nefertari's temple. We were once again astonished at the beauty of the amazing and still intact artwork and the overwhelming energy that we felt. No pictures are allowed inside so as not to damage the beauty that has preserved there for thousands of years. I explored every detail of this temple and saw fleeting visions of many gods and goddesses. Each would last only a second, but I was mesmerized.

I somehow knew the best place for my meditation would be at the temple of Ramses, not in Nefertari's temple. So we completed our tour of Nefertari's temple and entered the Temple of Ramses.

The interior of Ramses' temple was just stunning, but the energy was even fiercer. I could feel something building, and I asked Nancy if she could feel it. She could. We walked to a chamber that had been used as a library and chapel. As we walked around looking at the inscriptions Nancy suddenly grabbed my arm and pulled me toward her.

She asked if I felt the energy. I closed my eyes and felt this enormous pair of wings around me. I felt this loving energy so powerful and so pure. I felt this powerful, intense vibration that I had never felt. Nancy said, "Just breathe and be with the energy." I started weeping heartfelt tears, tears of joy, of pain, of excitement and of release. I was home. I just sobbed and then got on my knees and bowed as it was all I could do in the moment. Nancy and I sat there experiencing a powerful being and energy. We felt wrapped in a blanket of pure light. I had never previously experienced anything like this. As two other people walked into the room, the energy abruptly stopped. We got up and looked at each other knowing what each other was thinking. We left the room to the tourists and walked to another part of the temple. I didn't know what to do next. Should I still attempt a root chakra meditation or had I already been given the message from this temple?

I found a corner and sat in silence for a few minutes gathering my thoughts and connecting to the Divine. I noticed that the root chakra was spinning fully and easily. Whatever we had just witnessed had basically cleaned us out. There was nothing left but peace, and I was clear that our experience at Abu Simbel was intended to powerfully complete our Egyptian adventure. Everything we had experienced now seemed to make sense.

Nancy found me in my little corner and was very excited about something. She pulled me to a tiny hole in one of the walls where there was some loose sand and said, "We are supposed to take some sand with us. They said so." We happened to have a zip-lock bag with us and Nancy put some sand in the bag for us to take home. We put our hands on the spot and felt a very palpable and vibrant energy. We stood there for a few moments and waited for the energy to dissipate. When it did, we knew we were done exploring the temple and made our way back to Athem to go to the airport. Later we found a small container for the sand and added it to our collection of rocks. We had gathered rocks from each of the temples we had visited, each rock having its own unique vibration. These would later be added to my collection of rocks from Greece and Pompeii.

Before we left Abu Simbel, I needed to make one final stop, the ice cream stand. "Ice cream" and "thank you" were the only two phrases I had learned in Arabic. It didn't seem right to be at this temple and not have ice cream, since I had had ice cream at EVERY other temple in Egypt.

As we waved goodbye to Abu Simbel, we thanked the gods for our experience and left for the airport.

As we waited for our flight to depart, we had all kinds of feelings about the journey that was ending. It was very emotional for both of us. We tried to put into words what we were feeling about the whole trip, but really couldn't do it... It had been an amazing journey in many ways. I was a bit confused by all the messages we had received and wanted to know how to interpret them. Angels don't work through knowing, so it was useless to try to figure it out. I knew it would all make sense when it was supposed to.

I slept on the plane nearly the entire way from Aswan to Cairo. Nancy woke me as we were flying over the desert. As I looked down I imagined how many souls had walked across it, and how peaceful it looked. It must have been and still must be something to walk through the desert by camel, donkey or on foot. The desert has a lot of stories and holds a lot of memories of people who have gone there. I wondered how many other temples, pyramids, tombs and artifacts remain hidden under these desert sands. I wondered what would be the next Egyptian masterpiece to be uncovered from the lost sands of the Sahara.

That night, Nancy and I had our final dinner in Cairo by the banks of the Nile River. We both had Lute fish, and I believe it was the best fish I had ever eaten in my life. It was so tender, so flavorful and cooked to perfection. We sat there recounting our adventures and looking back at all we had accomplished and all we had left behind. Neither of us wanted it to end. Yet we knew that there were many things waiting for us to deal with when we got back to the States. I knew that Nancy and I would be having many more conversations about our trip as well as creating things for the future. This had been the first step in a new life I was creating for myself.

We packed and repacked to fit all our clothes and new purchases in our bags and went to bed grateful for the days we had had in Egypt.

Chapter 47

We arrived at the Cairo airport about 6:30 am for our flight back to New York. When we checked in, Nancy had no problem, but when I checked in, the ticket agent thought my flight was only to Frankfurt, not NYC. I told him that I was ticketed to New York. He looked at me, shrugged his shoulders, and said, "OK." Of course, I didn't think anything of it.

We did some final shopping at the Cairo airport and found our first Starbucks in Egypt. I was so elated -- Starbucks! It had been a long time since we had indulged in Starbucks. So Nancy and I both enjoyed our drinks and finished them just as we began to board.

When we got to Frankfurt the chaos began. When we checked in, we found out my flight to New York was cancelled. I was confused since I had booked both mine and Nancy's at the same time. Now I understood why the agent in Cairo had asked me if I was only going to Frankfurt. We found out that my flight from Frankfurt to New York had been booked for the previous day. Obviously, that made no sense at all. I had to be at work and was being told the next available seat was in three days. I could not imagine being stuck in Frankfurt for three days. I mean Frankfurt was beautiful and all. Rather, I had a fear of calling my boss and saying, "Guess what. I am stuck in Frankfurt and will be home on Wednesday." I didn't think that would go over well. We argued and argued with the attendant from Lufthansa, and I became more and more furious.

Nancy, the person who was there to keep me grounded, reminded me to ask the angels to help me. Oh right, the angels. In my anger I'd seemed to have forgotten all about them. Nancy was even willing to give me her seat on the plane and stay in Frankfurt until she could get another flight. I appreciated it, but I did not want her to do that. We asked Angel Chamuel to help us find a flight.

A few minutes later, I had a seat on the flight I was supposed to be on. Thank you, angels. However, my seat wasn't with Nancy. I happened to notice that right next to me was a row with two seats for handicapped people, so there was plenty of legroom. I asked the flight attendant if we could move to those seats after everyone was aboard, and she said yes. We were sitting together and had plenty of leg room for our Trans-Atlantic flight. The angels had come through again. Thank you, Angels.

We arrived back in New York safely and the next day went right back to our daily lives. Out trip had stirred up all my thoughts about the future. I began to confront what I would actually do if I left my job. I was drawn to pursuing my career as a healer but I wasn't sure how I would make the leap from a secure job to one I would have to create from nothing.

Chapter 48

Over the next few months I kept asking myself the same questions I had been having the previous year. "Who am I?" and "What am I here for?" The free expression I had felt in Egypt was a long gone phenomenon. I felt a heaviness, and I knew there was more to life than this.

The first week of October I flew to Laguna Beach, California to spend time to think and reconnect to the angels. When I first arrived, I met two women, Kelly and Julianne, at the airport who were going to the same hotel as I, the Surf and Sand. So, we shared a taxi. Kelly and Julianne and I were a part of a group that was coming together to study, talk, learn and experience the powers and healing of the angels. It was something I had read about and wanted to do for a while but never felt it was the right time. I was clear, this moment in time, was the right time.

We met a few others right away; Regine, Denisha and Megan, and we all became fast friends. We shared our experiences that evening during dinner. It was so freeing to trust and speak with another person about angels and not have that person think I was crazy. We laughed over fairies and their mischief; we laughed over the angels; and we laughed at each other. We created a bond that has not been broken. We shared about our different healing abilities and our knowledge of various disciplines.

Over the next few days, we did a lot of work with the angels. We did a lot of chakra clearing, a lot of block removing and a lot of visualization. We also practiced doing angel readings on each other and relaying messages from the angels. It was great to be with people who could do readings like I could. It was also great to receive readings rather than give them. Together we creatively challenged our clairvoyant abilities.

It was so great to add a whole new circle of people who share this love and connection with the spirit world. I felt very encouraged to move toward a life as a lightworker and healer.

Our room over looked the ocean and each night, we would sit outside and just hear the waves roar. Our visions got clearer as we saw images of angels over the water and a mermaid on a rock. It was fascinating to have these moments be so clear. I felt like I was so blessed to be here and blessed to have this new community of friends to share it with.

Every morning I would get up at the crack of dawn, about 6 am, and walk on the beach to a rock that we called the "Manifestation Rock." Supposedly, if you sit on the rock and focus on your desires, you will clearly get the answers you need to make them happen. I don't know how much that was true for me, but the "Manifestation Rock" definitely had a strong and palpable healing energy. The rock was down a ways on the beach and full of natural amethyst and crystals that had formed there. The rock was big enough for several people to climb and flat enough for all of us to sit on.

I would listen to my music as I walked to the "Manifestation Rock." I sat there balancing my chakras and visualizing what I wanted in my life. I asked the angels to bring clarity to the many messages I had heard in the past and did not know what to do with. As I sat listening to my music I heard Arch Angel Raphael loudly and clearly say, "You are a world renowned workshop and spiritual teacher. You will travel the world making a difference for the masses." Well, that was a little bit bigger than what I had thought for my life. I responded, "Ok Angels, if you want me to have that and be that, you have got to show me the way," and I left it in their hands.

Every day I pulled an angel card and every day I got the Energy Healer and Spiritual Leader cards. "Ok, now that makes things a lot clearer!" I thought, sarcastically. I decided that everything would play itself out; it always does. But at least I had something to work with. I now knew that I am supposed to be a leader but wasn't sure how to get there. All of the questions were running through my mind, but the only answer I got from the angels was, "Patience. Have patience. You will know what to do when."

A few of the readings that we did with each other were very interesting. Several of them said to begin to wrap up my job and move on. In one session, someone actually spoke with my grandmother, the grandmother who had told me that seeing the spirit world was not good. Her message to me was how proud she was of me, and how sorry she was to have told said things that suppressed me. She also wanted to know if I would forgive her. I had already forgiven her a long time ago but it was reassuring to me to hear those words.

Susan and Robin, who I would reconnect with again later, both did a reading on me and got the same message that I needed to live near the water. That was not a surprise since I had been thinking the same thing, but resisting it.

Susan did a reading first and saw me living near the ocean and playing with the dolphins. Robin also got that I had a huge connection to Atlantis and, in fact, she saw me as her teacher during that time. That made sense because she had felt a strong connection to me from the moment we had met. She shared with me her vision of me in Atlantis, and it turned out to be the same vision I have had of a temple with a crystal sphere and laser beams. The more she described this, the clearer I got that she was with me during that time.

When it came time to return to New York, I did not want to leave. The ocean was calling me. The energy was inescapable, and I had the same experience as when I had left Egypt. I had been exposed to a whole different world, and now I was having to go back to "reality."

This time when I got back, I could not deny that I had to start transitioning into a lightworker career. It was scary to make that transition, but I knew at some point I would have to do it.

Chapter 49

It began to be really hard to be in my job when my heart and often my mind were somewhere else. I was calling on the angels over and over to give me the strength, to give me the courage and to guide me through. It wasn't at all that I hated my job, I didn't. It just was no longer an expression of who I wanted to be in the world.

I talked to Nancy and Denise about it every day and also with my friend Chris who worked with me. I knew in my heart of hearts it was time to move on, but I was still uncertain that I could have a career as a lightworker. It became critical for me. I was starting to get sick a lot and just didn't want to go to work.

Every New Year's I do a ritual of making a collage and writing out everything that I am creating and want for the next year. When I looked at the finished collage for the upcoming 2008, it had a lot of spiritual growth, it had a lot of travel to places like Hawaii and Mexico, and it had a lot of swimming. It also had a lot of art and a lot of creative aspects. But it didn't have my current job represented. I knew at that moment that it was time to say something to my manager. I loved the company I worked for; I had worked there a total of 6 years and it had made such a huge difference in my life. I had grown in many ways and had extensive training, but I really felt it was time to move on.

In the beginning of January of 2008, I told my boss that it was time for me to do something else. He hated to see me go but understood. It was truly a tough choice for me, and it was a choice I knew I had to make.

As soon as I made that choice and really stuck to it, I started having more people call me to guide them on a spiritual path. I had begun doing healings, workshops, teleclasses and readings prior to leaving my company, but I became much busier as soon as I left. It really is true that as one door closes, another opens.

Chapter 50

In February 2008, my father was admitted to a hospital with possible pneumonia. He had not been feeling well for a while and was noticeably, incredibly tired, irritable and grumpy. As he was about to be released from the hospital, it was discovered he had a much bigger problem, congestive heart failure. He was rushed to a hospital in downtown Birmingham where he lives and was scheduled for immediate open-heart surgery with a quadruple bypass.

I left New York immediately and flew to Birmingham to be with my family. I asked the angels to help and called on Arch Angel Raphael to be with the doctors. I knew my father was going to be ok but it was still a shock for me.

My family and I did a lot of waiting before, after and during the surgery. I was a rock, grounding and keeping my family's sanity intact. When my father's surgery was complete, we were able to visit him in the ICU.

I stood by his bed envisioning a green light around him. I could see Arch Angel Raphael's energy weaving in and out of him. I put my hands out sending him Reiki and every other kind of energy healing I know. He was doing well and expected a full recovery.

He was released a few weeks later and his health since then has improved with velocity. I knew the angels would take care of him and pull him through. Thank you, Angels! It was confirmation that the angels send us healing power when we ask.

Right after I had gotten back to New York, I had fallen on the ice and heard my foot crack. I knew something was amiss as it hurt like crazy to walk on it. I didn't think it was broken but something was wrong. I had an x-ray done and was told it was fractured. It seemed every time I create a new beginning, or a new future for my life, something happens to my legs or ankles! I know that leg represents the ability to move forward in my life, but what was the message for me this time?

After a few weeks of wearing a boot-like cast, I was told it was inevitable that I was going to need surgery. I thought about it and didn't like that option at all. It was a hairline fracture for crying out loud! I knew I was going to Hawaii in about 7 weeks and I was not interested in walking on the beach with crutches. I asked Arch Angel Raphael to work his magic, and I did what I knew to do as well. I also called on my healer friends around the world to work on me. I could feel the green healing energy weaving in and out of my ankle.

Two weeks later, I went back to my doctor who said he had made a mistake. I didn't need surgery at all. Thank you angels! I got my cast of and went on my merry way.

Chapter 51

The last day of my job was in April of 2008. I had arranged that completion date so that I could attend a much needed vacation in Hawaii. I had never been to Hawaii and had heard of its magical powers. Three days later I was in Kona on the Big Island of Hawaii resting, relaxing and figuring out what was next for me. I was clear I needed to write, but I was not sure what would be first. I had started writing a book but was blocked. I also wanted to create and write workshops, but on what? It looked like the message that Arch Angel Raphael had given me in Laguna about being a world spiritual leader and teacher had started to come to fruition. Little did I know how soon it would happen.

While in Hawaii I worked on writing workshops and the ideas I would like to teach. I did some energetic clearing and took some time to explore the island a little. The volcano had started erupting again so I was not able to get near it. Pele, the Hawaiian Goddess, was throwing a temper tantrum. You could feel her fierce energy throughout the island.

I received a lot of information about what I was supposed to be doing with my life and having the courage to start it. Could I really make it happen? I still really wasn't sure in what direction to go with it all, but that was the reason for this short trip to Hawaii. I designed it to be a time for me to reflect, relax and rethink my life. It was also a time for me to connect with the angels again.

I sat in the ocean at Wiakoloa Beach and just let the waves run over me. The water was a bright blue and the perfect temperature for swimming. I stayed in it for hours. I just let the waves take my troubles away. I had memories again of Atlantis and just sat and let the ocean heal me.

The water was warm, clear and felt so soothing and purifying. I knew I needed more than anything to be in and near water but it's hard to just pack up and leave a familiar, comfortable life. I closed my eyes and asked the angels to guide me and take all my concerns away. The more the waves surrounded me the more peaceful I felt.

The trip to Hawaii had been short but a very relaxing and healing and much needed one. I had let go of a lot of the turmoil and fear of leaving my job and was now ready to begin a new direction for my life. I also knew I was coming back to Hawaii in October, so I let go of any regrets over what I had not had time to see and do on my first trip to Hawaii.

Chapter 52

Three weeks after I had gotten back from Hawaii, I was on my way to Cancun, Mexico. My father had invited my family there to celebrate our family and his victory over the heart failure. My sister Kayla, my step mother Toni, my father and I boarded a plane to beautiful, sunny Cancun. The angels had done some amazing work on my father in the past four months. He looked healthier than I had seen him in a long time. He looked younger and he looked more peaceful. His sense of humor was back, a side we had not seen in a while. I sat next to him on the plane and we had an interesting conversation about Atlantis, UFO's and other unexplainable events. We had not really talked about that kind of stuff before, and I felt for the first time he was starting to get my world.

In Cancun, I spent much of my time sitting on a veranda overlooking the pool and the beach and sipping frozen drinks. I used this time to write some workshops and contemplate my life's direction. It was a whole new beginning, and I could create anything.

I spent a lot of time in the water, swimming, snorkeling and relaxing. My body really wanted to be in the water and since it was perfect weather, I didn't argue.

My sister Kayla, and my stepmother Toni and I went snorkeling in an underground canal in the Mayan River. It was a lot of fun, and, again, I felt like I was back in Atlantis. Later I went by myself to a different canal, swimming in a cave that was pitch black. There was no light to lead the way. It was very scary, and I was very alone. I called on the angels and asked them to help me. Suddenly I was able to move peacefully and fearlessly among the fish.

We went snorkeling one day out among the reefs where schools and schools of fish came to me. There must have been hundreds of different fish swimming around me. It was like I was a mermaid swimming in the deep with all my fishie friends. I dove down and played around with them, and they stayed by my side. I looked around and realized that not only was I away from the group, but no one in the group had fish around them like I did. There must have been 100 or more. I felt like I could stay there forever. The mermaid in me kicked in, and I wanted to be in the water all the time. Every time I got in the water I felt so happy and free. I had forgotten how much I loved snorkeling and being with the fishies and how long it had been since I had done so.

Chapter 53

During our vacation in Cancun, we included a day at Chitzen Itza, (or as the Mexicans called it, Chicken Pizza) the Mayan sun pyramid. It was amazing to visit this pyramid and know that, even though no communication could have occurred, the Mayans and Egyptians had each built their pyramids at about the same time. It was also fascinating that Chitzen Itza and Saqquara Pyramid in Egypt were almost exactly the same size and in appearance. It was interesting to learn how the Mayan pyramids and structures been configured and laid out so mathematically.

I could feel the presence of the Mayan. It was an intense, dark presence. Not a bad or negative presence, just intense. We learned more about the Mayan calendar, and how they calculated the end of the calendar in 2012. They were spiritual in their own way and had a huge connection to the Divine. The intensity in their art was amazing and comparable to the Egyptian hieroglyphics.

What amazed me the most was the similarities between the Greeks, Romans, Egyptians and Mayans. They were all on the same wavelength, thousands of miles away, on other sides of the world and creating similar language, structures and theories. They each had multiple gods and goddesses that guided and supported them. There was a deep connection to spirit and a deep connection to self. They all received similar information from similar sources.

The trip to Mexico was profound in many ways. I felt connected to my family, I experienced being a mermaid, and I felt the love and power of the ancient Mayans.

Chapter 54

The day before I left New York for Mexico I had noticed a few small bumps on my right ankle, close to where the melanoma had been before. It looked like razor burn so I hadn't thought anything about it.

A week after I had gotten back from Mexico the bumps were still on my ankle. I showed them to Nancy who said they were nothing. I looked at them again and realized I should call and have the bumps looked at. My scheduled follow-up appointment was in July about 6 weeks away, and I wasn't sure I wanted to wait that long.

My doctor saw me the next day and looked at the bumps. There were a few more bumps around my lower leg including one near the spot where the melanoma had been removed. He was a little concerned and said it looked like it could perhaps be more melanoma but wanted to biopsy it to be sure. We scheduled an appointment for the following Monday.

It was a long weekend waiting for the biopsy to happen. I kept asking the angels to help me and to keep me sane during the next few days. To take my mind off of it, I spontaneously went to Atlantic City with my friend and housemate Tony. We were able to keep my mind clear and have some fun, and I even won some money in the process!

On Monday, I went to the doctor at 9 am for the biopsy. I was nervous, scared and numb. I tried to keep a good face but eventually it gave way. I waited about 30 minutes for the biopsy results and then went back to my Doctor's office with the results in a folder under my arm. He brought me into the office and said, "Well, you definitely have a melanoma again, and it is not good." I then asked, "Am I going to die?" He paused for a moment and said, "I don't know. I am going to send you upstairs to an oncologist who will work with you further. I am not pushing you off, but I am a surgeon, and she knows more about possible treatments than I do."

I burst into tears. I could not hold it back any longer. I made my way upstairs to the oncologist and waited to see her. I called Nancy and she did not pick up the phone. I texted her an urgent message. I called Denise, and left a message for her too. I even left a message for Mary. Where was everyone? The surgeon had sent someone up from counseling services to be with me and help calm me. I waited for hours to see the doctor. I finally spoke to Nancy who reminded me that I had the power to say whether or not I was going to make it through this.

The oncologist's intern came in and examined me thoroughly. There seemed to be no other apparent bumps in my lymph nodes, in my breast, or anywhere else on my body. The counselor stayed with me throughout my doctor's appointment and helped me think of ways to laugh and to bring light to the situation.

Finally the oncologist came in. She was very nice and I immediately liked her. She gave me a lot of reassurance that I was not going to die. She said, "The good news is that you will be with me until I retire, and the bad news is that you will be with me until I retire." She then looked at the biopsy report and said I needed to have surgery soon. The procedure I would need to have would be a critical procedure, called Limb Perfusion. I would have a surgery during which chemo would be infused into my leg for several hours. I would be hospitalized for several days. She said there was an 80% chance it would be successful. If it wasn't, she would have to look for other options. She seemed very confident, however, that this procedure would work.

She referred me to one of the top cancer doctors at Memorial Sloane Kettering Hospital in New York, one of the best cancer centers in the world.

I called my father, Nancy, Denise, Chris, and many others and let them know the news. My friend Mary, who had been such a help when I had the first surgery, had called me back to talk to me for a while. She always knows the right things to say and was still one of my angels here on earth. I tried to be calm, but underneath I was really scared.

I had a lot to deal with. That night, I contacted all my healer friends from around the world and asked to be put on prayer lists and healing chains. I asked them to do any kind of healing work on me that they could. As much as I was telling and assuring people I was not going to die. I had this huge fear that my time was limited. I knew I had to be strong, not only for my friends and my family, but also for me. I spent lots of time talking to people to keep my mind sane and to keep me from believing I was going to die. I was grateful for all the support I was receiving from around the world. It was great to know that I was in the hands and prayers of so many. I knew that the angels would have everything turn out and all would be well in the long run, but I didn't discount any sources of healing that were available to me. I laid the crystals on and around my leg, I meditated and did everything I could to calm my mind.

Chapter 55

I had to take a series of tests before I could even go to meet with the doctor. I had to get different types of blood tests, have a cat scan done and get a full chest x-ray. Then I had to traipse around the city to get all the results to take with me to Sloan Kettering.

On my way to Sloan Kettering, I got a call from my oncologist saying that the cancer was absolutely in no other location in my body. YAY! This was the first good news I had in days. What a relief! I felt lighter and more together.

My friend Chris was meeting me at Sloan Kettering to be my ears for what the surgeon had to say. I had found from my past experiences, that it is always better to have someone with me at one of these key appointments. It provided a great relief to have him there, with the additional benefit that he could note anything the doctor said that I would have trouble remembering due to my anxious state of mind. When we got to Sloan, we were greeted with more tests before meeting with the doctor. I was annoyed. I just had those test done and the results were in my bag but, apparently, the doctor needed both.

Chris and I waited and waited and waited. Finally after what seemed like hours, we were called back to see the surgeon. When the doctor finally came in, she gave us the lowdown on the procedure that she would be doing, the Limb Infusion. Basically, she would put a tube in my leg and infuse chemicals. The procedure would be minor and take about an hour. Hmm, it seemed longer and more intense when my oncologist had mentioned it. I would only have to be in the hospital overnight. Now, I knew something was off, because I distinctly remembered my doctor saying I would stay in the hospital for several days.

I asked her about the statistics and she got quiet. She said, "Well, there is a 50% chance it will work and an 80% chance the cancer would return." This did not sound like what my oncologist told me. I was a little agitated and said, "That doesn't work for me. What else have you got?" She looked at me for a moment, not sure what to say, and then proceeded to mention that there was another procedure that a doctor at the University of Pennsylvania could do. It was similar but it would be a much more intense procedure. It was a six- hour procedure and much more serious, but the documented results were better. She didn't seem thrilled that I was even considering that. We went ahead and scheduled a date for the New York surgery, and I would get the second opinion from the surgeon in Philadelphia. Should I take the second opinion, I would cancel the New York dates.

When I left the hospital, I was shaken. I called my friend Glenn, who is a cardiologist in Philadelphia. I asked him if he knew anything about the doctor, the hospital or the procedure. He didn't, but said that a mutual friend of ours, Angela, worked at the University of Penn, and he would call her. Within minutes, he called me back and had Angela on the phone.

She actually knew the doctor and worked closely with him and because of that was able to schedule an appointment for the following Wednesday. I was so grateful. Glenn talked to me a few minutes and told me to keep him updated. During this whole battle with cancer, Glenn has been right there at my side. I am very lucky to have him to talk to.

I called my father and told him what the doctor had said and that I had an appointment scheduled in Philadelphia. I would ultimately choose where I would have the surgery after meeting with the second doctor.

That night I was doing an Angel Party, which is a party where I do several angel readings for people in a party - type setting. I kept flashing back to my day with the doctors and had to keep having the angels clear my mind. I called on Arch Angel Jophiel, the angel of beauty and grace, to bring me her calming energy and to help de-clutter my mind. It was great doing those readings because as each reading came through, I took the message for myself. The angels were definitely guiding me, healing me and giving me strength.

Chapter 56

As I anxiously awaited my appointment in Philadelphia, I spent a lot of time on the phone with people who were out to have me have a positive attitude and go into this with peace of mind. I had created a team of people who were available to me for whatever I needed.

I was supposed to call them if I got scared, if I was upset, or for whatever I needed. This team consisted of Mary, Karen, Herma, Nancy S (not my "Egyptian" friend Nancy) and Kristi. Margot, who had also supported me the first time, made herself available 24/7. She was a retired nurse and could provide answers and comfort that I needed. They are all powerful leaders and powerful women who are trained to have transformation and power happen, no matter what. They also bring compassion, comfort and love in times of need. Nancy

S. and Karen live in Philadelphia, and Mary, Herma and Kristi are from New York.

There were moments that I felt great, moments I was scared, moments when I had freedom and power, and moments when I felt hopeless. I tried not to let it show; however, those closest to me could always pick up on what I was going through.

I talked to the angels every night and every time I had a thought of something. They kept saying, "Trust. We have this one under control. You will be fine."

I set up a final call with my team to have me clear and grounded before I went in to see the surgeon. They gave me the opportunity to really say anything that was going through my mind, including my fears about the surgery and about dying. By the end of the call, I felt relieved and calm. This is just what I needed and that support was what kept me going, having a team around me made all the difference in the world.

Chapter 57

I didn't sleep much the night before I went to Philly, as you could imagine. I had to be on the 7 am train for my 11 am appointment. One of my friends and team members who lived in Philadelphia, Karen, met me there. She was both a melanoma and breast cancer survivor and had many words of wisdom for me and was a great help with my doctor. She knew the questions to ask, what to listen for. I was so grateful she was there.

We were greeted by our friend Angela and seen very quickly by the doctor. He looked at my bumps, which in a few weeks had gone from five bumps near my ankle to about twenty bumps on the lower part of my leg.

This surgeon was one of the leaders nationally in this particular procedure. He said that the procedure would take about six hours. This was not the first time I had heard this, but the length of the surgery was still shocking to me! I would be in recovery for about an hour after that. He would put a tourniquet on my leg and infuse chemo into my leg, then flush it out with oxygen at the end of the surgery. The point of the procedure was to concentrate the chemicals only in my leg where the cancer was located and to keep it out of the rest of my body. That sounded really smart to me.

He said I would be bedridden for about 3-4 months, and that he expected I would regain almost full flexibility.

I tried to imagine ME being bedridden that long. I am always going, going, going and this was a really long time to be immobile.

He felt like I was a great candidate for the procedure. He said that there was about an 80% chance the surgery would work and a 20% chance the cancer would return. That was a much better statistic than the 50% success rate of the Sloan Kettering procedure. He said that we could schedule the surgery for the first week in July.

Although I liked the odds much better, I had to consider several things. I would have to do the surgery in Philadelphia as opposed to New York. All my friends were in New York so I wouldn't have them with me. I would have to stay in the hospital for 3-5 days as compared to one night and the recovery period seemed very long.

Karen was with me when I called my Dad. She was able to tell him the things that the doctor said that I didn't remember. Both the tentative New York surgery and the Philadelphia surgery were scheduled during the first week of July which was only three weeks away. I needed to choose pretty quickly. Would it be Philadelphia or New York? The surgery in Philly had better odds, but all my friends were in New York and I would have to travel back to New York after this big surgery.

My father said he would come to whichever hospital I chose. It was up to me. I thought about it and thought about it and settled on Philadelphia. I figured the statistical difference alone was worth it. My father said he would get a room in New York City so that when I returned from Philly my friends could come see me, just like they had for my first surgery. This made me a happy camper.

I had enormous support from my friends and family in my decision and thanked the angels for guiding me to a doctor that would have it all work out. It even turned out that my oncologist in New York had always wanted me to have the procedure that was being done in Philadelphia. She hadn't realized that Sloan Kettering did not do the Limb Perfusion procedure.

Chapter 58

The next few weeks leading up to the procedure were trying for me. I talked to Denise everyday and Chris every day, as well as my "team" to create and keep a positive outlook. I spent a lot of time with Nancy too, both on the phone and visiting her in Connecticut. I would call her in tears and she would get annoyed with me. I didn't understand why this good friend, who had been so great in the past was now being so annoyed with me. We finally realized that her job with me was to support me in being happy and positive. She was not the person for me to go to when I was scared or upset. That was a job for my support team.   After we got that straightened out, there was a real clarity around who I should go to for different kinds of support.

During this time I went to see the musical, *Cry Baby*, on Broadway and when I left, I was sad because I had the thought that this might be the last Broadway show I would ever see. Nancy said, "Well it could be the last one. You could get hit by a bus tomorrow." Her silly humor always got to me and I laughed. She definitely didn't allow me to be sad or significant.

The laughter helped a lot but it didn't stop the waves of emotion. They would hit me like a ton of bricks. One minute I would be fine and then BAM, without warning, I would be a sorry sack of tears.   But despite my waves of emotion and fear, Nancy kept finding ways to make me laugh.

I kept saying to the angels, "I don't want to die." But I never felt freedom. I still had that gut wrenching feeling that I could not shake. I begged the angels and Arch Angel Raphael in particular, to heal me. I envisioned him shining his green blanket of healing energy around me.

I kept telling Nancy, "I didn't want to die." She would always say in response to my saying that, "Then don't." One time while I was visiting her in Connecticut, she began to look up at the sky and got this look she gets when she is about to get a message. She said, "Ok, it is up to you. The angels are saying if you want to die, you can. If you want to live, you can. But it is up to you." I sarcastically thought, "Well! That's comforting! Come on angels, give me more than that." After all I the work that I had done with the angels I was pissed.

I looked at Nancy and said, "I don't want to die. I want to live." Nancy said, "Oh my God, you have been saying you don't want to die. Change your words to you want to live. You know the words you speak create the world you live in. You are a master at language. Besides, you can't die. I need you for Egypt next year. You are not going to leave that to me, no way."

I forgot that in the Law of Attraction, the Universe doesn't respond to the word don't. Nancy suddenly began laughing and saying, "The angels just laughed. They say you have already healed. You have no control over it. You have a choice, but you have no control. They are laughing at you." I smiled and realized the angels are laughing at me a lot. I must be a handful for them.

Once I changed my thoughts to "I want to live", the fear disappeared and I knew that all was well. I felt lighter than I had felt in a while. I felt the energy shift, and I knew the angels were with me, albeit they were laughing, and I knew everything was going to be ok. I took a deep breath and sighed a sigh of relief. I was now ready to continue the rest of this journey with some freedom and power.

Chapter 59

The day finally came for me to go to Philadelphia for my surgery. I had to be there at 8 am the day before the surgery for pre-op tests. My always amazing Dad had booked a room at a Marriott in Philadelphia for us. The hotel wasn't that far from the hospital so he would be able to stay there comfortably while I was at the hospital. I left my apartment at 5 am with suitcase in tow and rode Amtrak to Philadelphia. I had just enough time to drop off my luggage at the hotel before rushing to the hospital.

My friend Angela greeted me in the lobby, and I registered with the administration desk. Angela must have pulled some strings because there was no waiting involved; I was done with the tests by 8:30 am. Nancy S from my team had come to be with me, but by the time she got there, I was done with my pre-op stuff and was ready to leave. Nancy, Angela and I went to have breakfast since I could not eat before pre-op tests and I was starving. After breakfast, Nancy and Angela went back to work and I went back to the hotel.

I spent the rest of the day walking around Philly. I was nervous but did my best to keep myself relaxed. I knew the angels were with me. My father was arriving around 4 pm that afternoon. We still didn't know what time my surgery would be. The nurse said that they call me with the scheduled time by 5 pm. So to distract myself until my Dad's arrival, I did one of the things that I do best, I went shopping.

I collect small fairy figurines and love going to Philadelphia because there are so many stores that sell fairy things. There is a cute little store on South Street called Mineralistic, and they have quite a collection of fairies, stones and many other things I find appealing. I found a green fairy that was beautiful. I could not take my eyes off of her. Something about that fairy was very healing to me. I told the owner of the store my reason for being in Philadelphia and about the surgery the next day. He gave me some crystals to take with me, a smoky quartz, an amethyst, and a hematite. All are powerful healing stones. I had brought some of my favorite crystals with me but I thought it would be smart to accept all offers of healing power.

My father got to the hotel about 5 pm, and I gave him a quick tour of the area. We grabbed a quick bite to eat and then went back to our room to watch TV. I talked to Nancy in an attempt to keep my mind off the surgery, but I was finding it difficult. The hospital called, as they said they would, and told me I should be there at 11:30 am and that surgery was scheduled for 1 pm. Rats! Why couldn't it have been earlier? I couldn't eat after midnight; I was going to be starving.

My sister Kayla called my Dad that night. She had really wanted to come to Philadelphia to be with me during the surgery, but she was only able to arrange arriving the next afternoon. She was scheduled to arrive around 6 pm, about the time my surgery would be done. She was going to come directly to the hospital and my father gave her directions. I talked to Kayla and my stepmother Toni for a few minutes and then took a hot bath. I stayed up and ate something at 11:55 pm. I knew that I would not be eating for a while so I enjoyed every last bite. Then off to bed I went.

Chapter 60

On the following morning, I woke up, took a shower and gathered my things all before 8 am. My friend Karen was joining my father and I for breakfast at 8:15. Well, they were going to have breakfast, and I was going to be watching. I watched them enjoy their breakfast buffet of eggs, fruit and pancakes and fantasized about my own meal after surgery. We sat and talked while I tried to calm my ever worsening nerves.

Karen and I went back to the hotel room. She told me it was ok to be scared. I told her my fear of not waking up after the anesthesia and she made me promise to come back. I promised.

We compiled a list of the people needing to know the results of my surgery. Karen would take care of updating my team, friends and associates. My Dad would call family. I wanted this set up so that there would not be a lot of people calling my Dad to find out what had happened. I knew that Nancy would be making additional calls and would update the appropriate people.

I gave Karen a hug and walked her downstairs. She said she would come down to the hospital after work, and I told her that I looked forward to seeing her.

My Dad and I hopped into a cab with some of my stuff. He would bring the rest of it as I needed it since I was going to be in the hospital for 4-5 days. I showed him the Starbucks near the hospital and said I would want a latte when I woke up.

I checked in for surgery at the registration desk and was, again, admitted fairly quickly thanks to my friend Angela. I changed into my blue paper hospital gown, slippers and surgical hat. My dad, Angela, the doctor and I met before I was wheeled to the operating room. The doctor reviewed the procedure with my Dad and told him he would let Angela know periodically how the surgery was going and would come report to my Dad when it was over.

I told the doctor on the way to the operating room that it was critical that he stay alert and positive during this procedure, that I had things to accomplish. He looked at me like I was crazy, but I told him I would do my part to come back and he has to do his part.

The next thing I knew I was in the operating room, on the table and talking to the anesthesiologist. He wanted me to take a few good breaths and then, boom, I was out like a light.

Chapter 61

The next thing I knew, the doctor was telling me it was six pm, the surgery was over and I was going into recovery. I could hear the people talking in the background but I could not open my eyes. I could hear the nurses laughing and carrying on about their lives, and I could also hear the nurses trying to talk to me.

I finally opened my eyes around 10:30 pm. I was so thirsty. I begged for ice. I begged for water -- something. The nurse periodically gave me a swab of water that had been frozen and I could suck the water off. This was almost as good as the ice cream I had when I was suffering from the heat in Egypt.

I asked for more water or ice, but apparently I was only allowed one drop of water an hour. Blah! Finally, they said that I could go to my room. I had been booked in a private room and was glad that the only people I would have to be with would be family, friends and my angels.

After about thirty minutes, I was in a new dressing gown, propped up with plush pillows in my bed ready to see my father and my sister. They had been waiting for hours for me to get out of recovery and were glad to see me awake.

I talked to them for a minute. My Dad said Karen hadn't come by since I was in recovery so long. He said that he had talked to Mary and Nancy and both knew that the surgery had been successful and I was recovering. He said that he wouldn't have me call them that night since I needed to rest but that I could call them the next morning when I woke up.

My sister, Kayla, briefly told me about her flight and then, they both kissed me on the head and went back to their hotel. It had been a long day for them. It had also been a long day for me.

Unfortunately, after they left, I was still wide awake. I was thirsty, and there were a lot of potential pain sites that were starting to bother me. I had 15 stitches in my lower calf where they had cut the muscle so it would not explode from the pressure of the chemo. I had two drains in my thigh, about five stitches in my stomach and about 26 stitches in my groin area.

My nurses gave me a drop of water and said they would be in the room with me all night in the event I needed anything. I needed water, but apparently no one was going to give me any.

I finally drifted off in a sound sleep waking up every few hours for my precious drop of water. The nurse had to pump the morphine pump for me because I was so knocked out and unaware. I remember waking up a few times to make sure someone was still with me, and then I went back to sleep. Finally about 6 am, I got more than one drop of water. I got about three. Yay! Life was good!

Chapter 62

I woke up about 8:30 am Friday morning and had a few more drops of water. It was so good! I looked out the window of my room to see Kayla and my father peeking in. I waved at them to let them know I was awake.

The only way I could sit up was to be propped up with pillows. I couldn't move, and I was really sore. The nurse came in and brought some water, some real honest to goodness water, more than a drop. My Dad held the cup to keep me from gulping the water. Agh! I was not supposed to have more than a few sips at a time or I might get nauseous. But it was sooo good.

My father had the nurse hook up the TV in the room so I could watch movies. I was going to be there for a few days so I needed some entertainment. The laptop and the books I had brought to use after surgery would have to wait. I was too tired to do anything that required much energy or focus.

We watched TV all afternoon. Kayla sat in a recliner, I was propped up in bed, and my Dad was in another chair in my room.

Karen and Nancy called, and though I could barely speak to them, it was great to hear from them. Nancy was checking my email and responding for my business as well as updating my website every day. She said I was making money while I slept. Hey that was good news!

Later that afternoon, I was able to have cranberry juice and it was soooooooo good. Juice never tasted better!

The nurses were monitoring my heart rate. It would jump up and race with the slightest movement. The nurse had said it was time to go for a walk. As soon as I sat up, my heart raced from 100 to 150 beats in about five seconds. I felt dizzy and lightheaded and weak. The nurse decided that I was not ready to venture out of my bed.

That night my body felt ready to eat something. I ate a bowl of green Jell-o and beef broth and another of raspberry sorbet. Yum! My Dad fed me because I didn't have the strength yet to feed myself. Right after eating the sorbet, I got sick. I guess I was not as ready to eat as I had thought I was. My Dad asked if I wanted my latte. I rolled my eyes and declined.

The nurses got me situated again and gave me my morphine pump. I said goodnight to my Dad and Kayla and fell asleep watching TV.

Chapter 63

I woke up the next morning when my Dad and Kayla arrived. The nurse helped me move to the recliner and had another one brought in for Kayla. I was given my medicine, had my drains and bandages changed and was given a quick sponge bath before breakfast.

They brought me food, my staples of cranberry juice, beef broth and green Jell-o. The nurse took my vitals and said I had lost a lot of blood during the surgery, and that I needed to have three units of hemoglobin infused. She said I would feel better in a few hours. So they hooked me up and let it drip.

I spoke to Nancy and she said I sounded so much better than I had the day before. I was still really tired and really in pain. Apparently, the lack of blood and the inability to move was getting to me. However, my spirits were high and I was asking the angels to help me in every way possible.

My nurse said I was the best patient she had and that she switched her schedule to be with me. She said I was the only patient that was intentionally creating wellness. Despite my pain, I didn't complain that much and she said I was always chipper. My father laughed when she said I was a delight. I stuck my tongue out at him, and the nurse and Kayla laughed.

Chapter 64

After about 2 hours, the first hemoglobin unit was finished and another one was put in. I started to slowly feel better and had more and more energy as the day went on. My Dad was gone on some errands and Kayla was asleep in her recliner next to me.

I was watching a movie on TV when I looked over to the left side of me and saw Arch Angel Michael over me. It was the first time I had seen him so clearly. It was as clear as a human being standing beside me. I did a double take. I thought for just a moment I was hallucinating due to the medication I was on. But I knew I wasn't. He was there to protect me and remove all fear related to my cancer, my surgery and anything else that was there. He wanted me to know all would be well. I took a deep breath and smiled. I felt so relieved. We were then joined by the strong presence and green, healing light of Arch Angel Raphael. I was totally comforted and totally at peace. I thanked them both for helping me. I could see the purple and green lights circling and surrounding me and reminding me that they were there. This lasted for about 30 seconds and then they vanished. Even though I no longer saw the lights, I felt their powerful presence and knew they were there.

I had been nervous about receiving the hemoglobin, because I didn't know how my body would react to it. So seeing Arch Angel Michael was a peaceful reminder that all was well and I was truly in the hands of the angels. I held my favorite crystal, a Lemurian quartz to calm me.

That afternoon after the remaining three units of hemoglobin were infused, and the fuel of my beef broth and green Jell-o lunch were consumed, I was able to go for a walk. I walked around the floor of the hospital for about five minutes. That was a big deal for me. I went back to my room and lay down. That was about all the exercise I could do for the day. My Dad and Kayla left early; They needed a break. It was my sister's first time to Philly, so my Dad was going to show her the sights. I sat in my bed and watched bad TV until my dinnertime broth arrived. I was able to slowly feed myself, so I was making progress!

By the evening, I felt much better and I was beginning to have hopes of going home soon. It all depended on how well I reacted to the hemoglobin, how much I could move and how much fluid was draining out. My surgeon came by a couple of times but the residents were the ones who really checked in frequently. They seemed pleased with the progress, although they had some doubts that I would leave within the next two days. Despite their doubts, I was creating it as a real possibility.

Chapter 65

I woke up Sunday morning determined to go home. It was my fourth day, and I was done with the hospital and the beef broth and the green Jell-o. I asked my nurse what needed to happen for me to go home that day. She was a little stunned. She was not my regular nurse, and she was not used to how I had been creating my day and my wellness. It was natural for me and very unusual for her.

She said that in order to be discharged, there were several things required. I needed to be able to get up by myself. Check. I needed to be able to feed myself. Check. I needed to be able to walk around the floor of the hospital with a walker. Check. So far it was beginning to look like I was good to go. The doctors came in and said I looked good and that I could go home, but I needed to go home with the drains still in. If I left before they were removed, I would have to come back soon to have the drains and the stitches removed.

Moving would be uncomfortable but I could deal with it. So the doctor gave me the clearance to go. As soon as the nurse completed the necessary paperwork, I would be able to leave. When my Dad and Kayla arrived, I gave them the good news. Hooray! I was going home! We checked the train schedule and found there was a 2:30 and a 3:30 train. We were aiming for the 2:30 train just because it would get us to New York earlier in the day.

The nurse gave me a bath and then showed Kayla how to empty the drains in my legs. I put on "normal" clothes for the first time in a few days. Although the drain bags looked like I had two hand grenades hanging from my thighs, I was still able to wear appropriate summer clothing, shorts and a tee shirt. I had one sock on and one shoe on because my foot was so swollen I could barely get a sock on it, much less a shoe. I was ready to go.

My father and Kayla took all our suitcases downstairs and waited while the nurse wheeled me out to the front of the hospital where we could catch a cab to the train station. We made sure we had some graham crackers and plenty of cranberry juice and water for the ride. I had a few pain pills to take in case the pain kicked in.

We were able to make the 2:30 train. I luckily had an empty seat to rest my leg on, which was really great. I asked the angels to help us make our connection in Trenton and promptly fell asleep. The next thing I knew my father and Kayla were waking me up in Trenton. Our train had been delayed in leaving Philadelphia, thus making it very likely that we would miss our connection in Trenton. Fortunately, the train in Trenton was also running late, so we made it without any stress or chaos. Thank you, Angels! I went across the platform and grabbed a place on the Trenton to New York train that was big enough for the three of us to sit together. Kayla slept while my Dad and I talked and looked at the scenery as the train rolled by.

We got into New York around 5 pm and took a cab to the hotel.

When we got there, I was surprised to find my friend and apartment mate, Tony, there to greet us. He helped me get up to the room and worked with us to get the room settled.

I had just gotten myself propped up in the bed, when I heard a knock at the door. It was Nancy. She had come to see me. Tony let her in and she visited a while with us. Tony left after about 30 minutes to go to an appointment.

Nancy kept me company while my Dad and Kayla went to get my prescription filled. She said she was really glad to see me and told me how she had worried when I was in recovery for so long. She asked me if I had had thoughts about staying with the angels while I was under the anesthesia during the surgery. I smiled... She laughed and said, "I knew it. You didn't want to come back. You wanted to stay where it was comfortable, ya big jerk. Well, thank god, you made that promise to come back." It was so great to have her humor. We laughed and had a great time catching up.

Dad and Kayla had to go to three different pharmacies before they could find one that was able to fill the prescription. When they came back, I was starving. So they went to get food -- pizza. I was so hungry for real food that I didn't care if my body was only used to broth and Jell-o. If I was going to throw up, that's just the way it was going to be. I didn't care. I wanted to eat!

Nancy stayed for a while visiting me and then left to go home to Connecticut. She called me on her way back, something she does often, and we chatted some more. I managed to eat the pizza and really appreciated having real food in my body.

That night, Kayla helped me make sure I took my medicine exactly when I was supposed to. I stayed awake for a bit and then crashed hard and fast. I had to rearrange myself a few times and let out yelps of pain. I could not yet roll over, and when I moved, I felt jabs of pain in my side.

I don't think that my father or Kayla slept well that night due to my whimpering like a wounded pup.

Now that I was not being pampered in the hospital, I got a good dose of reality. I had to relearn to walk long distances, I had to have help getting in and out of bed, and I had to have help with a bath. I had temporarily lost my independence.

Chapter 66

Over the next few days, my Dad and Kayla, took care of me, helped me eat, bathe and walk. But then came the time when they had to go home to Alabama.

So they transported me out to Queens via New York City taxi and then did enough grocery shopping to set me up for the next couple of weeks. I had them buy a lot of spaghetti and sauce. It just sounded good.

Princess Zoe was terrifically glad to see me. She immediately crawled into my lap and purred and purred and purred. Tony was glad to see me too. Maybe he didn't exactly crawl into my lap and purr, but he was very glad I was home.

As my Dad and Kayla prepared to head to the airport, I started to weep. I don't know if I was weeping because they were going or because I was tired and in pain. It was probably a combination of both things. The 20-minute trip to Queens from the hotel had worn me out and I was just frazzled.

Later that day, my home nurse, Geralda came to see me. She was an amazingly gentle woman who had a lot of compassion for my weeping ways. Now it was time for the real healing to begin.

Geralda came twice a week to see me and helped take care of me. Given I was pretty much bed-ridden, it was great to see her and have company other than Tony. Every night Tony would ask me what I wanted for dinner and every night I would respond, "Spaghetti." It got to the point he would ask me if I wanted "the usual," to which I would respond, "Yeah." I ate spaghetti every day for two weeks, long enough for Tony to worry that I was either going to turn into pasta or start speaking Italian.

I do not do bed-ridden well. I had to have help getting off the couch, getting out of bed and eating meals. I had to be wakened for scheduled medication, and I slept a lot. I became grumpy and irritable with the irregular schedule and the dependency -- Tony needed a break. Chris, my friend Marianne, and many other friends came over to spend time with me and help Tony in supporting me.

I spoke with Karen or Mary every day. They let me share with them what I was dealing with. The thoughts of dying came and went, and they worked hard with me to keep a positive attitude present.

I was out to do everything I could to further my healing. So I kept talking to Karen, Mary, Nancy and Denise every day. Chris came to see me often and we would watch movies, eat lunch and laugh. Every day I would make sure I watched "The Ellen DeGeneres Show" to amuse myself. One of my friends would always make sure I was awake so I could see it. Laughter was the best medicine. Tony was out to have this healing be fun and happen with velocity.

I kept my healer friends in the loop and kept my family and friends updated. I slept with crystals by my leg and on my Biomat, a healing mat made with Amethyst and Tourmaline. Zoe would lie on my lap and put her paw where I had my incision. Even she was out to heal me.

Chapter 67

Over the next couple of weeks, I did a lot of healing, mentally, physically, emotionally and spiritually.

Two and a half weeks after my surgery, I was scheduled to go back to Philadelphia for a check-up. Although I was essentially supposed to be bedridden and not supposed to be traveling, I set off for Philadelphia on my own. I still could not get a shoe on my foot and it was a long ride. I had to be there at 11 am for the appointment, so I had to leave really early with pain pills in hand. It was a trek just getting into Manhattan to catch the train, much less getting to Philadelphia. It took something for me to climb the stairs of the subway to get into the train station and then walk to the train. I could feel the pain creeping in.

By the time I got to Philly, I was in a lot of pain. My foot was the size of Montana, and I still had to go back to NYC later in the day. The thought of spontaneously renting a hotel room in Philly became really appealing.

I waited and waited to see the doctor. When he came in, he had great news. He was amazed at the healing I had caused in only two weeks. The bumps had gone down drastically, and he was thrilled with my progress. He went on and on about my healing and was stunned it had happened so quickly. He said it looked like the surgery was a success and that he felt confident I would recover fully.

Much to my disappointment I only had one of the drains taken out of my leg. I was hoping both drains would be removed and my stitches taken out, but he told me I would have to wait two more weeks.

After my appointment, I made my way back to the train station. I made it on time and was able to find a seat where I could put my foot up. My Dad was in New York on business and I was going to get to stay with him at the hotel again. I could not wait to get back to New York, get some food, get to the hotel and see my Dad. I was taking pain pill after pain pill to ease the pain. I called Nancy, Denise and Karen to give them the good news about what my doctor had said. They were all very excited and happy. Knowing that I was healing and moving in the right direction took away a lot of my fear and stress.

I met my housemate Tony at Penn Station where he handed me my overnight bag. To keep me from having to drag my bag with me to Philly and back, we had arranged for him to bring it to me on his way to an appointment. What a huge difference that made! He was such a hero during all of this. From Penn Station I took a cab downtown to the Marriot in the Financial District and called my Dad on the way so he could meet me when the cab dropped me off. The cab driver screwed up and dropped me off across the street from the hotel. I had to hobble across with my luggage, cane and swollen foot.

When my Dad and I got up to the room, I could not move another step. I hurt badly. It had been a long, trying day. The skin around my foot was cracked and chunks were falling off from the swelling. I would leave a trail of chunky dead skin behind me whenever I got up to take a walk. It was pretty gross. The doctor said this was a short-term result of the chemo and, ultimately, it would cease.

The next morning, I was going to run an errand and get my father a particular treat that he likes. I made it as far as the lobby. The pain was just too much, and I went back up to the room crying tears of pain and frustration. It was then quite clear to me why they had said I would be bedridden for 4-6 weeks minimum. Despite my frustration, I stayed in the room all day. This was not going to be easy for me. When it was time for my father to go to back to Alabama, he dropped me off at my house in a cab on the way to the airport. He helped me up the stairs to my apartment, and I went back to bed. Again, the ride home had exhausted me. I was starting to learn that the cost of going out, even for a short time, was three days back in bed.

Chapter 68

Every day I worked with Arch Angel Raphael to heal and nurture me. I visualized his healing blanket around me. Every day I used crystal energy. Every day I talked to Mary or Karen. I began creating and creating -- creating my business, creating my health, creating peace of mind. I was determined to have nothing slow me down.

Denise and I created our day every day. Nancy and I created ideas and plans for our individual businesses. We started planning our next trip to Egypt. That kept me going. I had something to look forward to. Whenever I got slightly down, she reminded me of the angel's help and their healing power. She also made sure I continued to laugh. She and Tony were convinced that I was healing with velocity.

My friends, Kelly, Julianne, Megan and Denisha who also work with angels, did a healing circle with me. I kept in touch with my friends from around the world who were healers or worked with angels and was getting healing messages from all of them. I was accepting all gifts.

Chapter 69

Two weeks later, it was time for my second post-surgery exam in Philadelphia. Even though I knew I would pay for the strain on my body later, I was happy to be getting out of the house.

I made my journey to Philadelphia fairly easily. It had been about four weeks since my surgery, and while I had been bedridden most of that time, I was still mobile enough to get around better than I had expected. I arrived at the hospital promptly in time for my appointment.

The nurse took out the stitches in my calf and put sterile strips over it. Then she took out the remaining drain. This was looking good! Then one by one, she took the stitches out of my groin.

Prognosis – unbelievable! She said she had never seen someone recover from this procedure as quickly as I was recovering. She was stunned and amazed as she checked my vitals and gave me two thumbs up. Thank you, Angels.

Then, I got some not-so-great news. She warned me of the coming pain. She said the pain would start kicking in very soon. Since the surgery had killed the cells and nerves in my leg, they would begin regenerating again soon. As they healed, the pain would begin. The more pain there was, the better the healing. She said that the pain would come in waves and might be rather debilitating at times. I was given a new pain pill specifically for that pain, and she said it could take up to a year for the nerves to regenerate fully. I would have to take the pain as it came. There was no answer to when it would start and how long it would last.

I had plans to meet my friend Karen later in the day, and we were going to have dinner to celebrate. I had some time to wait before she was to pick me up so I thought about going to a movie or anyplace where I could sit down. I decided on Barnes and Noble.

I had some tea and grabbed a couple of books, found a chair and got all comfy. I was so wiped. I took a nap right there in Barnes and Noble. I must have slept for about two hours when Karen called and said she would be there soon.

I gathered my things, paid for the purchases and went downstairs to meet her. I could still hardly walk and moving around was a real challenge. But I was so happy to be out in the world, that I would gladly have suffered just about anything.

It was a nice dinner with Karen. I had not seen her since my surgery. We caught up, and I gave her the good news about the speed of my recovery. Hooray! Later on I caught a train back to New York. I was worn out. I was in bed for the next few days after this adventure. One day out, was still several days back in bed.

Chapter 70

About a week later, the pain started. It felt just like pop rocks being poured down my leg. Pop Rocks are a candy that was popular in the 1970's. When you put them in your mouth, they popped and sometimes created a stinging sensation on the roof of your mouth. The pain was like that, and when it hit, I could not move. It was uncontrollable and got so bad at times that all I could do was hold my breath and cry.

I would beg the angels to help me. I would have Tony rub my foot and my leg. I couldn't take a salt bath for another week and I was counting the days. It had been five weeks since surgery, and I had missed taking a hot bath. The mermaid in me felt very landlocked and I was so looking forward to replenishing myself with the salt water. I was getting antsy.

My friends were very patient with me during this time. Mary and Karen were, as always, very supportive and Nancy made me laugh. When my doctor had said I could not go through this alone, boy was he right. I had a team of people near me and in many countries supporting and healing me. I had empowering conversations, books, movies, art and various healing modalities touching me and inspiring me to keep pushing through.

It was very trying period. Sometimes the pain was incredibly bad and then other times I would go days without a single burst of pain.

I was tired pretty much all the time. I had to schedule and take naps frequently. If I didn't schedule them, I would forget that my body needed the down time and the rest. It was difficult to need to sleep so much because my mind was clear, but my body was tired. I had to keep reminding myself of what I had been through and to take it easy. My primary job was to heal myself.

Chapter 71

It was September now, about two months since my surgery, when I went to the doctor in New York. It was my first doctor's appointment with my oncologist since the surgery, and I was nervous.

Chris went with me to the doctor's office. We waited and waited and waited. Finally after about 3 hours of waiting, the doctor saw me. I was apprehensive and anxious to hear the news.

She greeted us with a warm welcome as she always did. I really liked her a lot. She looked at my leg and like the doctor in Philadelphia, was amazed at my recovery. She took pictures of the bumps that were remaining. There were 30 bumps originally on my leg and now there were 23. Seven bumps had disappeared completely, and of the 23 bumps remaining, 60% were in the process of disappearing. Amazing news.

She was stunned and happy, saying I was about a month ahead of schedule. I was walking pretty well and without a cane at this point. YAY!!! The angels on earth and in spirit had really done an amazing job.

I think for anyone who didn't know how I looked before the surgery, it would have been hard for them to tell that I had had major surgery only two months before.

My doctor reminded me that I was still a prime candidate for a clinical trial vaccine that might come up. It was not yet approved but when it was I would be considered.

I had a lot of questions to ask her. The most important one was regarding my upcoming October trip to Hawaii.

I had booked the trip a year ago and was really looking forward to it. I had been counting the days ever since my first trip in April. Was I going to be able to fly?

She looked at my leg and said I could go. YAY! YAY! YAY! I had been so concerned about that. She told me I would have to apply a specific type of sunscreen. Agreed. I would have to wear a compression sock. Agreed. And, I would have to rest as much as possible. Agreed.

For now, the only exercise I could do was swim. The good news is I could swim as much as I was able. So while I was counting down the days until I went to Hawaii, I would swim and swim and swim at a local pool.

Swimming was interesting. I kicked one way and my foot and leg went another way. I had no control over my foot or my leg, but, I was back in the water. The mermaid in me was getting ready for the adventures in Hawaii.

Chapter 72

October 2008, Three weeks after my doctor's appointment I was on a plane to Kona, Hawaii for the second time that year. We had been doing all the healing work I could do to prepare. I had gotten the clearance from my doctor to fly, had bought my ticket and was on my way.

I was going to heal, have fun, connect with friends and take my skills as a lightworker to a new level.

It was my first time flying since my surgery and I was a bit nervous. I had promised to call Karen when I got to Hawaii and to speak to Mary every day to make sure I was healing ok and didn't need anything. It was really, really great to know that I was being supported and taken care of even on the other side of the globe. I also promised them that I would have this be the most fun and healing vacation ever.

I landed in Hawaii about 7:30 pm. It had been a long day of flying. I had had delay after delay and was wiped out, swollen and hungry.

I dropped my things off in my room and met Charmaine and Debbie from Australia. I would be sharing a room with them part of the time while I was there. They were quite fun and very funny and I knew instantly we would get along.

I went to the hotel bar overlooking the water. There were giant Manta Rays swooping back and forth eating the plankton that was being drawn in by the big spotlights that hung overhead. I watched for a few minutes amazed at the grace and dignity with which they moved through the water despite their enormous eight-foot wingspan. I named the manta rays, Charlie, Fred, Bertha and Howard. It gave them character. We even called ourselves "Charlie's Angels." It became part of our evening ritual to say goodnight to Charlie and crew.

As I left the bar to find some dinner, I ran into my friends, Susan and Robin, that I had met in Laguna Beach the year before. They had just arrived and were going to be doing the same healing workshop that I was. I had known they were going to be here but had not talked with the recently. As soon as we saw each other, it was as if we had never parted. And, better yet, they had food! I was famished! I sat down and finished off the remainder of their appetizers and enjoyed their company for a while. We talked about how excited we were to be in Hawaii. We spent some time discussing the angel work we had been doing and the direction our work in general was heading. We enjoyed discovering how much we had grown since the last time we had seen each other.

After about an hour, I decided it was way past my bedtime. I was tired, and it was 3 am New York time. I didn't want to risk overdoing on my first day.

I got back to the room and Charmaine and Debbie were already asleep. I changed clothes and took all of about three minutes to fall asleep. I dreamed of the Hawaiian breeze, the ocean and the wonders it had in store.

Chapter 73

The next morning, Charmaine, Debbie and I had breakfast on the terrace overlooking the Keahou Bay. The sun was shining and it was an exciting time. I introduced them to American cereal and they introduced me to Australlian phrases. We were meeting together with a group of people from all over the world to work on and develop our skills as lightworkers.

We were all lightworkers and healers who connected with angels in various ways, and we had set aside this time to get together to grow and support each other. It couldn't have been more appropriate given the economic crisis that was happening and the upcoming presidential election. We felt that the planet needed some healing and the work of lightworkers. We were happy to be of service.

We were also spending time working on and developing our mediumship skills at a new level. Charmaine and Debbie were like little fairies running around. They made me laugh so hard. We were definitely visited by the fairies while we were there. I could sense their playful energy and mischief the moment I got there. We laughed and laughed at the pranks that the fairies played on us. The fairies, not Debbie and Charmaine, hid my shoes in the drawer and hid my money. Charmaine and Debbie and I spent so much time laughing at each other and the antics of the fairies, that I almost forgot I had recently had surgery.

Charmaine, Debbie and I met with Susan, Robin and a few others and talked about our ability to decipher and receive the messages from loved ones who had passed. We all had this ability and were working together to gain clarity in both our work as a medium and the various healings and readings we were doing already. We also wanted to enhance our work in all areas of being a lightworker. It was being overseen and mentored by a well-known medium and author who worked with us and enabled us to really master and develop our own style and skills. She was a great contributor to us all. We not only learned a lot from her, but her validation of what we already knew was a great boost to our self-confidence.

Our resistance to learning, speaking to the deceased, and owning our power as lightworkers grew weaker, and our bond with each other grew stronger. Together, we worked through many issues including past life and current life traumas. We had to manage how open we were to the many spirits that wanted to talk to us   Sometimes when we were "off duty," we would ask them to go away.   And they did.

Chapter 74

I loved the powerful, peaceful and beautiful energy of Hawaii. I loved the sunshine, the 70 degree temperature, the beautiful lushness of the landscape and the fresh pineapple. I loved the way the ocean roared and the sweet smell of the ocean's salt air. I felt so alive, so vital and so relaxed, and this was after only two days of my 14-day trip.

We spent some time cleaning our Third Eye and removing any debris or gunk that might be clogging it. What was seen by others in clearing my Third Eye was fresh pineapple, the blue waters of the ocean and that mermaids don't like to live in New York. Well Duh! I could really see myself living in Hawaii. It felt like home and really resonated with me. I felt the healing vibration of the island around me. Pele was at her best. The vibration was so healing you could sit on the lava and feel a deep penetrating energy. The sunshine was always good and the pineapple, oh my, was the best. I could eat the pineapple every day!

I also got the message that new and exciting things were coming to me. Big things, but I wasn't sure what. It seemed that the angels liked to have things come in big packages for me. Every journey I had been on had had given me the message that something "Big" was to come out of it and I grew exponentially. The message I received this time from the angels was one that I had received many times before, "Relax. Trust. Everything will work itself out. You will know what is next, and you will know what direction to go in." It was a message that had rung true the many times I had heard it before. No matter how many times I had heard it, it still left me with the question, now what?

Chapter 75

I was very fortunate to be in the company of so many avid healers of so many modalities. I had shared about my having the melanoma and that it was such a big deal for me to come to Hawaii at this time. I wanted to take advantage of not only the beauty that Hawaii has to offer but also take advantage of the amazing healing that can take place there. One of the people in our group suggested a mass healing for me.

They got together and put me on a couch by the water and each performed their own unique healing ability on me. This went on for about 20 magical minutes. People did variations of Reiki, of sound therapy, and many other practices that were new to me. It was so peaceful and relaxing. I could feel the vibration of the energy around me, and I could hear the peaceful waves of the ocean in the distance.

I felt as if I were floating and out of my body. Someone sang in German to the bumps on my leg and told them to go away. I felt the swelling and pain diminish in my leg and in my whole body. My mind started to clear and any thoughts I had of leaving this planet were gone in an instant. It was one of those moments that anyone would want to have last forever.

I had experienced a massive creation of energy. There were energy swarms of angels and ascended masters around me. I felt the love of the angels and I knew I was going to be ok.

Chapter 76

The next day was a day of power, healing, and total self-awareness. It was my first of two days of swimming with the dolphins in the wild blue Hawaiian waters. I was so excited I could hardly stand it. I had been waiting for this since the first time I was in Hawaii. I had always felt a connection and love for the dolphins and now I was going to be in the water with them only inches away from me.

We left the dock at 8:30 am. We got to the marina and did a nice invocation that was peaceful and heartfelt. There were ten of us on board plus the captain and her crew. Jeanie, the captain's mate, asked "Who are the swimmers who are not going to want to get out of the water?" I raised my hand before she could finish the sentence. I had been in Hawaii five days and had not really been in the water yet. I was craving the salt water of the ocean and needed to get in soon.

We boarded the boat and set sail. Within minutes, there was serious dolphin action. There must have been nearly 200 dolphins swimming, jumping, and flipping around the boat. It was terrifically exciting. We were surrounded by spinner dolphins and about every five minutes they would jump and spin out of the water. It was magical! Every time I tried to take a picture, I would just miss the shot. They were so fast! While I did end up with some extraordinary pictures of my dolphin friends, I mostly ended up with lots of pictures of splashes – no dolphins in sight.

I could hardly contain my excitement. It was finally time to get in the water. YAY! YAY!! YAY!!!. There were dolphins swimming all around me, beside me and underneath me. It was utterly, incredibly amazing. I felt so at home and I felt the mermaidian tendencies start to arise. I floated there in awe at the gigantic creatures around me. I was home. This was the life! I knew I could stay here and embrace this moment forever. Coventina, the Celtic goddess of the sea sprites was with me. I knew she would bring her connection to the dolphins and her ability to heal to my swimming.

I swam with the dolphins and watched as they played and spun around me. There were mamas and babies around me everywhere I looked. They were laughing and playing. There was no fear on my part and no fear on theirs. We were connected.

A few minutes later I experienced this horrific pain in my leg. I gasped. The pain was so intense I thought I was going to black out and would have to get out of the water. We did not have life jackets on so if I blacked out, it would not go well. I had not had this much pain before. I took a deep breath and happened to look down. I had 13 dolphins swimming right beneath me in a circle. I instantly relaxed, for I knew they were using their sonar to heal me. I just let them do their thing and within moments the pain was gone. I also felt the energy shift when they went away. They circled me for about 5 minutes before swimming away together.

Before I knew it, there was another pod of dolphins around me, scanning me, playing with me and healing me. It was so remarkable I didn't want to get out of the water. This mermaid was happy as a clam. As far as I was concerned I could spend the next part of my life swimming with the dolphins every day. It was one of the most fulfilling and rewarding experiences of my life.

A few days later, I got to do it again. This time it was at sunrise. We took the boat out and I could not wait until I was able to swim with my friends again. This brought in so many Atlantean memories and vibrations. I felt relaxed and at home. Once again, the dolphins amazed me with their immediate connection to me. I felt like I was let into their secret world. There were no worries in me as I connected to that part of me that is the ocean.

The days I did not swim with the dolphins, I snorkeled in the bay near Keahou in Kona. Having schools of fish swim up to me was another confirmation for me of my perfectly natural desire to be in the water. I saw all kinds of fish; Angel Fish, Clown Fish and many more of the local tropical fish. A giant sting ray swam under me as well. I panicked for a moment but took a breath, and relaxed, watching the beautiful creature beneath me. I also saw my favorite fish, the Money Fish. As I was snorkeling, I looked down and saw what looked like money. When the ripples of the water settled, I saw it was money. I took off my snorkel, dove about 12 feet and grabbed a brand new sopping wet $20 bill! Yee Haa!

I snorkeled almost every day in the bay. I found it to be very healing and relaxing. One day, a Hawaiian Sea Turtle befriended me during my snorkeling adventures. We swam for about 20 minutes together over and around each other. He let me take pictures of him as we swam over and under each other. At the end of our time together, he put his nose to mine as if to say "Bless you, until we meet again." Several other turtles joined me in a swim while I was in Hawaii, but none seemed as special as the one in Keahou. It was magical.

Chapter 77

I spent as much time in the water during that two weeks in Hawaii as I could. It was healing and cleansing and I definitely felt like I needed it. There was something that happened in swimming with the dolphins that I can't explain. I am not the same person now because of it.

On my last day there, I sat on the lava overlooking Waikoloa Beach and the tears just started streaming. I knew that a chapter was ending in my life and there was a new one beginning but I didn't know where it would take me. My heart felt like moving to Hawaii but my business and my friends were all in New York. I wrote in my journal and just let Pele' the Hawaiian goddess nurture me. I asked the angels for guidance as I have many times before. After a few moments, I looked up and the way the clouds and sun had come together, it looked like an angel standing over the water. I knew that was my answer. Trust the angels.

I left that night on the midnight flight to New York. I had never gotten on a plane and cried when I left a place. I looked at all the people I had connected with, both for the first time and from the past, and reveled in the experiences of being a mermaid and swimming with the dolphins. I had connected with people who would be in my life forever. We would continue to grow together, heal together, create together, and connect with the angels together. They are people who understand me and can appreciate what it is like to be a mermaid out of water.

Chapter 78

Two days after I had arrived in New York, I went to my oncologist to make sure that I had no clotting from flying and that the bumps had continued to disappear. I waited nervously to see the doctor, not sure what she would tell me. My housemate Tony went with me.

The oncologist was truly dumbfounded at my progress in this few short weeks. Of the 30 original bumps, I had only eight remaining and they were all dead cell space. This meant that the cell was dead underneath but the spot where the tumor had been had not yet disappeared. These spots, at the rate I was healing, would disappear very quickly. This was good. Very good.

The next thing she said with a blank stare. I braced myself for bad news. She said, "I don't know your secret and I wish I did, you are over 2 months ahead of schedule. There is no possible way, medically or physically, that you could heal as fast as you are. It just isn't possible. "

I smiled to myself. I knew the secret. I thought of all the conversations I had had with Mary and Karen and the others on my team to remove the fear and keep a positive mindset. I thought of all the times I laughed till I cried with Nancy. I thought of all the times that Chris and Denise had been there pushing me forth and never letting me get down. I thought of Tony's commitment to my healing with fun and velocity. I thought of my family supporting me and never giving up hope. I thought of Kristi staying on the phone with me until the wee hours of the morning. I thought of the many other people who fought for and supported me. I thought of my daily practices of crystal energy, Reiki and healing. I thought of the dolphins and fish swimming beneath me and around me. I thought of all my new friends and my experiences in Hawaii and I thought of my friends, the angels, in "high places."

It has been said that, "it takes a village to raise a child." I say it takes an army of angels, both in the spirit world and on earth, to raise a human being.

Chapter 79

This is my story. It is a true story. It continues to be one of healing, hope, courage, inspiration, and determination and never giving up. It is a reflection of who I am, and who I strive to be. It is a lesson in being true to oneself, no matter what circumstances life hands you. It is about discovery about embracing the various journeys that life has to offer and never looking back.

It is about allowing people to love you, heal you, nurture you and contribute to you. It is about teams. It is about being a spiritual being. It is about the difference one person can make. It is about friendships, new and old and about creating dreams to fulfill.

It is about living life to the fullest and not being stuck with anything other than something extraordinary. It is about trusting yourself, and your guides. It is about being open to all the miracles that life has to offer, big and small. It is about having fun and exploring the world you live in and exploring the world out there.

It is about not stopping and not settling for less than a miracle. It is about laughter and music. It is about discovery and adventure. It is about anything being possible.

It is about having a human experience and making the most of it.

It is about you.

About the Author

Heather is an Indigo Child and a powerful lightworker who works with others to awaken their spirit through teaching, meditation, healing and love. She has created Healings, Workshops and Sacred Journeys to awaken and elevate the soul's vibration.

She has been an intuitive healer for over 20 years. She was declared a Reiki Master at the age of 13. Heather currently lives in New York City and has led workshops and trained thousands of people in various life-altering topics. She is currently working on global projects and is developing a new training and certification program that will be released in 2009.

Heather has a vision of healing and giving hope to the world. She sees the world as such a powerful place, full of unlimited possibilities. Her mission is to evoke and wake up as many people as possible to the amazing life that awaits them.

WEBSITE : www.sacredindigo.com